Content

Introduction

For many people Barry Island is synonymous with sun, sea and sand, and certainly has its place as a part of the great British tradition of the seaside holiday. Barry Island came to prominence as a seaside resort around the end of the nineteenth century, when the island was joined to the mainland, and began its ascent towards becoming the holiday destination of choice for families from around the south Wales area and beyond, where it provided generations of working-class holidaymakers with a sunny retreat from the constrains of everyday life.

Despite the fact that that Barry Island was not the archetypical seaside town replete with a grand pier and neat rows of elegant Victorian hotels and houses – such as existed at other Welsh seaside resorts like Aberystwyth and Llandudno, or in English resorts such as Brighton and Blackpool – Barry Island could nonetheless boast two sandy beaches, a fairground, and a host of quintessential seaside amusements such as donkey rides, Punch and Judy shows and boat trips, as well as providing such seaside culinary treats as candyfloss, ice cream, and fish and chips.

Barry Island's popularity reached its zenith during the middle of the twentieth century, culminating with a Butlins holiday camp being constructed on Nell's Point in 1966. The authors themselves have many fond memories of times spent at Barry Island beach as

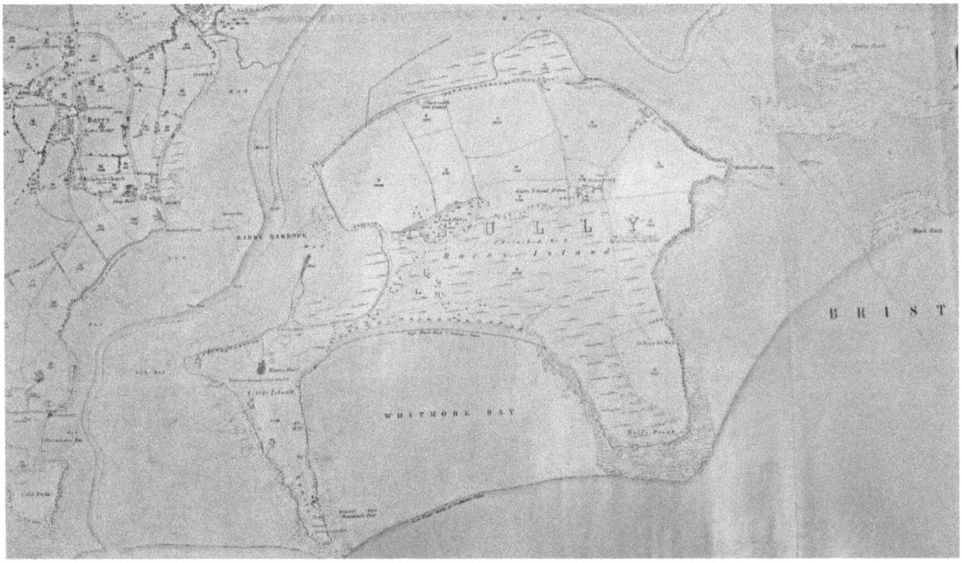

Victorian map showing Barry Island and mainland before development. (Source: Glamorgan Archives.)

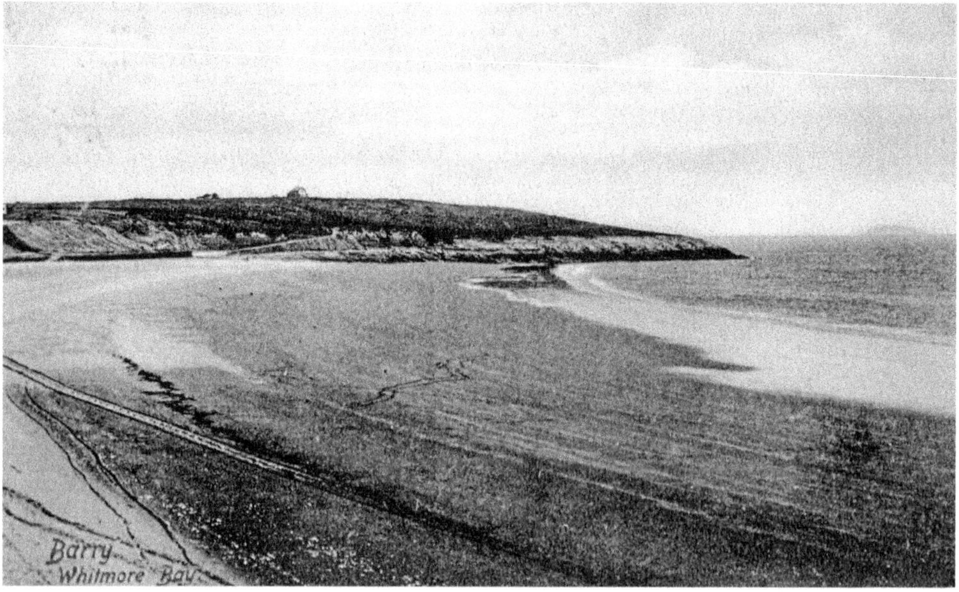

Late nineteenth-century photograph of Whitmore Bay. (Source: Tom Clements.)

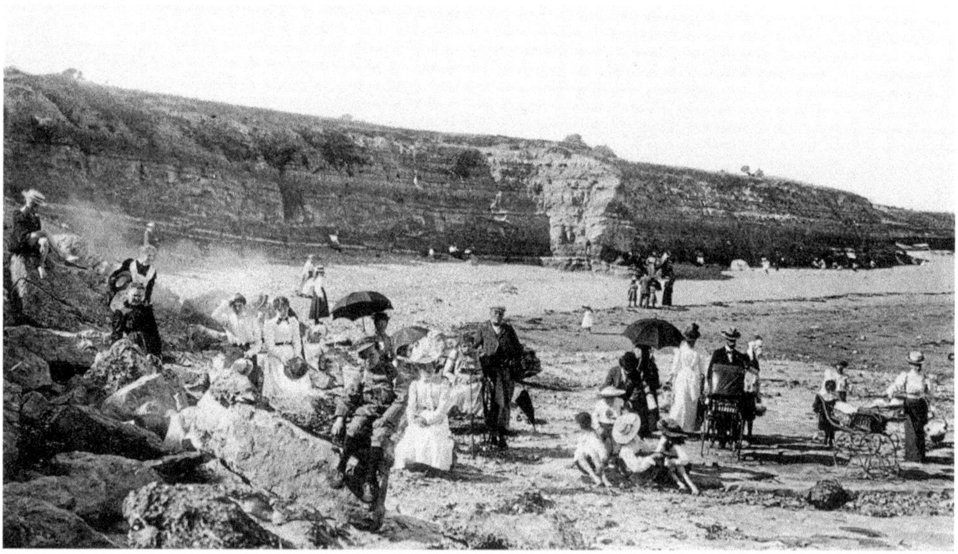

Edwardian tourists enjoying a day out at Whitmore Bay. (Source: Tom Clements.)

children, building sandcastles, eating ice cream and visiting Butlins; no doubt many of our readers will also have similar nostalgic recollections about their time spent here.

Sadly times have changed: the advent of the package holiday, which gave ordinary Britons the chance to visit exotic and far-flung parts of the world, helped cause the decline of the traditional British seaside holiday. Barry Island, it seems, was not immune

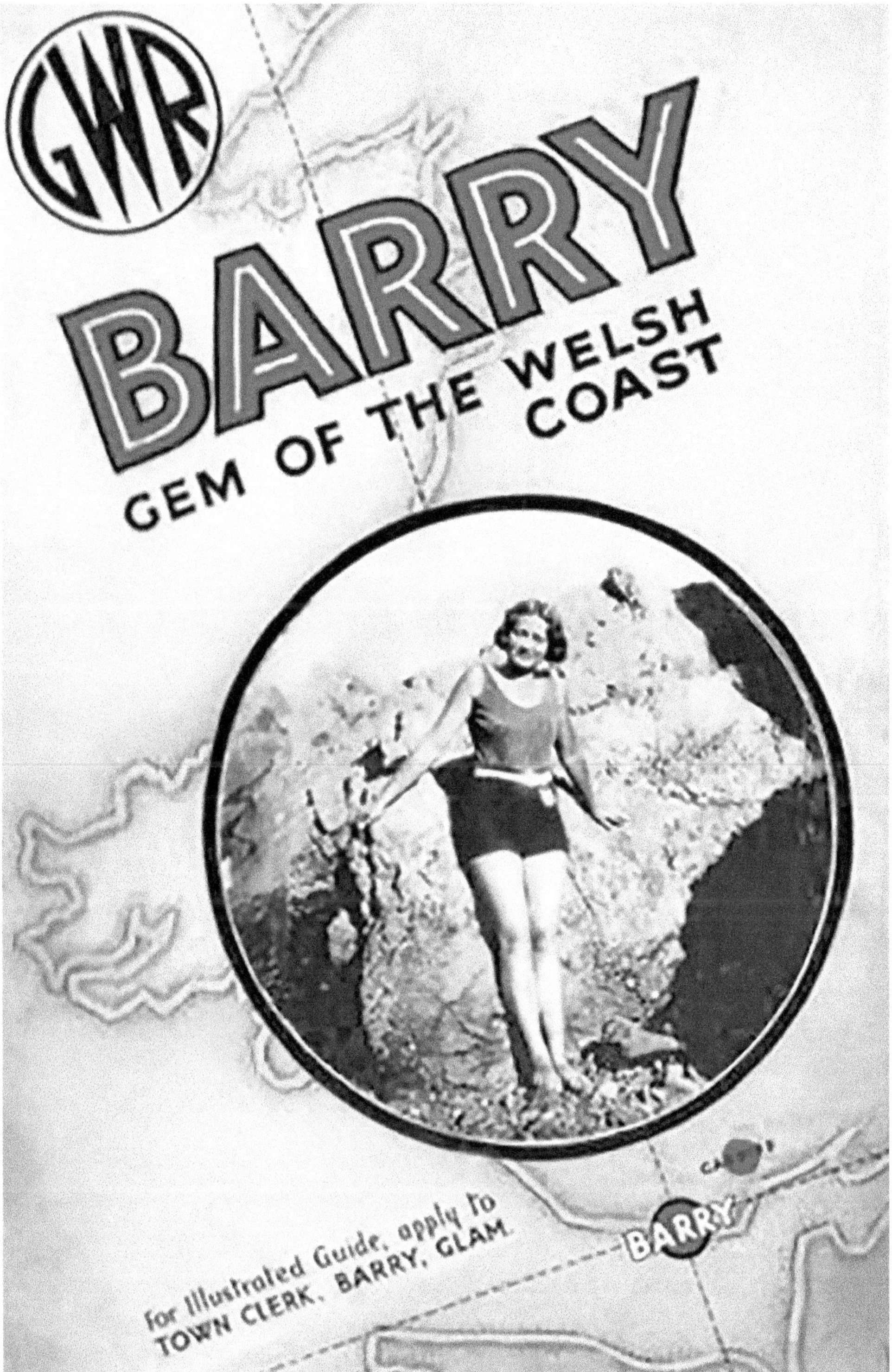

Poster advertising Barry Island as a popular seaside destination. (Source: Old Barry in Photographs.)

from this decline. Butlins and the later Majestic holiday camp have both been and gone and the tourists seldom arrive in droves as they once did. While Barry Island's profile has enjoyed a recent surge due to its location being used in the popular TV show *Gavin and Stacy*, it nonetheless lives in the shadow of its former glory years. This book, however, is not overly concerned with the island's heyday as a holiday destination, trains, or indeed the island's twentieth-century history; much like the sands of Whitmore Bay, this is all well-trodden ground. This book aims to reveal a far more elusive and distant history.

Barry Island is located in the Severn Estuary approximately 9 kilometres south-west from the city of Cardiff within the boundaries of the modern county of the Vale of Glamorgan. It is around a mile and a half in circumference, containing approximately 170 acres of land. Barry Island is comprised of a variety of geological strata including Carboniferous limestone, much of which is ruggedly exposed on both Friars Point and Nell's Point, as well as Keuper Marls and Rhaetic Conglomerate from the Triassic and Jurassic epochs.

Barry Island contains two promontories: Nell's Point located on the south-east side of the island and Friars Point located on the south-west side. Sandwiched between these two promontories is Whitmore Bay. This fine sandy beach has been attracting day trippers and holidaymakers for over a century and is responsible for turning Barry Island into a popular holiday destination. Barry Island also contains a second, albeit smaller, sandy beach called Jackson's Bay, which is quite often overlooked in favour of the larger and more picturesque Whitmore Bay. Jackson's Bay is located on the south-east side of the island, wedged between Nell's Point and Redbrink Point.

To the west of Barry Island is Watch Tower Bay. Although not a popular beach for tourists, it nevertheless contains a sandy beach endowed with a substantial Victorian period breakwater that was built to help protect the docks from the tides of the Severn Estuary. This bay is flanked by rugged coastline and the old harbour, an obsolete port on the mainland dating back to at least the thirteenth century. Watch Tower Bay is abruptly

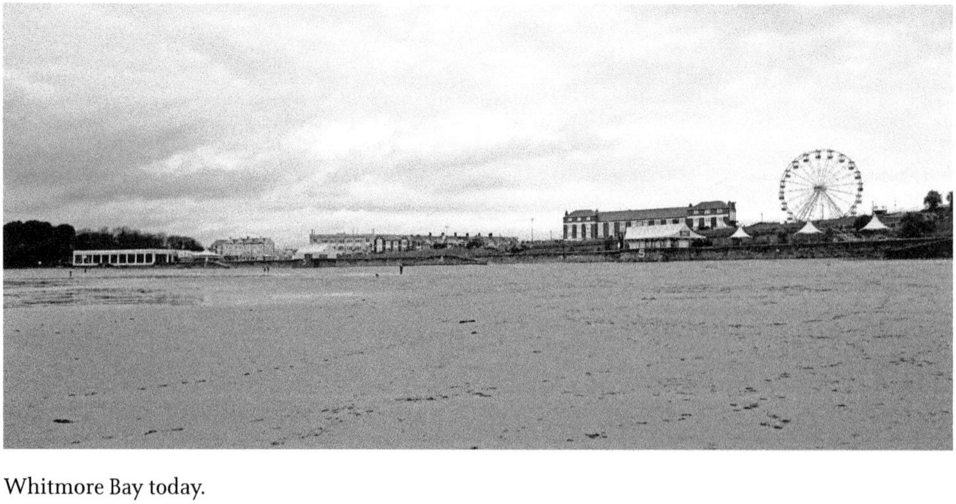

Whitmore Bay today.

terminated with the dam that forms the main road into Barry Island; incidentally, it is this area where boats visiting the old port used to moor. To the north-east side of Barry Island lie the docks. Constructed in the late nineteenth century over Barry Sound, this construction effectively sealed Barry Island to the mainland, giving it the appearance it exhibits today.

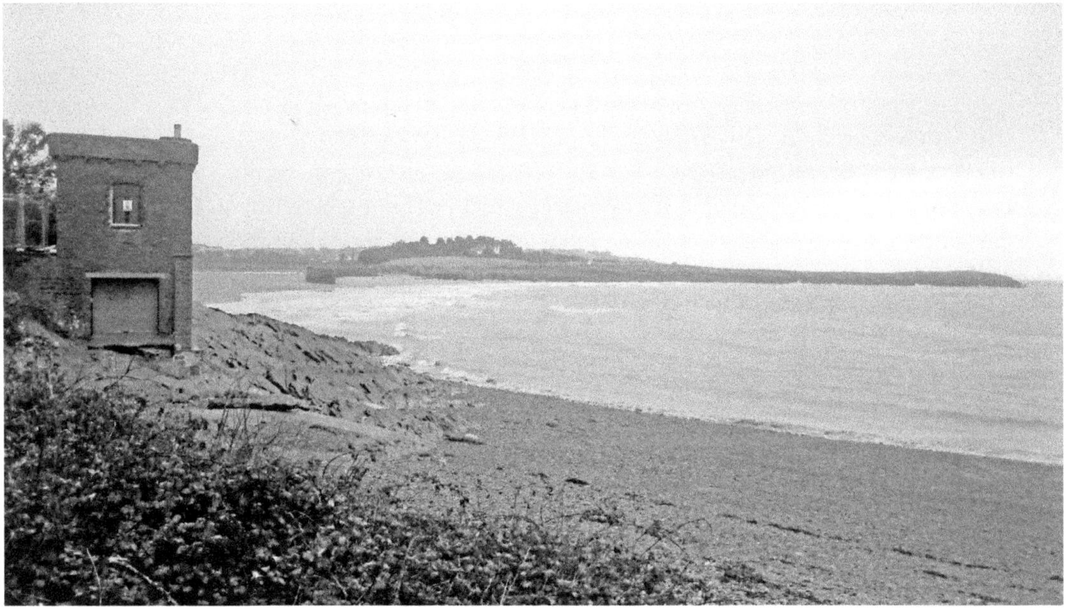

View of Watchtower Bay.

1. Early Accounts

A great deal of Barry Island has been covered with modern developments, such as housing, since the island was joined to the mainland; in fact, with the exception of Friars Point, one would be hard-pressed to find many places on Barry Island untainted by modern construction. Yet despite its cluttered appearance as a peninsula to the modern town of Barry, Barry Island, as its name suggests, was once an island and would have looked very different to the appearance that it exhibits today. The island's character and appearance would not have changed much from prehistoric times until the period the island was developed to cater for tourists and day trippers.

DID YOU KNOW?
Although the name Friars Point has been in existence from at least the late eighteenth century, there is no evidence for a friary having existed on Barry Island.

An early description of Barry Island's geographical setting comes from William Camden in his 1586 work *Britannia*. He describes the island's situation as:

> Scarce three miles from the mouth of the River Taff, in the very winding of the shore, are two small but very pleasant islands, divided from each other, and also from the mainland by a narrow frith. The hindermost is called Sully, the farthermost is called Barry.

The Revd J. Evans, writing in 1804, further describes Barry Island's geographical setting:

> The Vale opens into a sandy estuary, which expanding to the right and left embraces the small island of Barry. The traeth or sands are at flood covered, and are as about as wide as the Thames at London Bridge. At ebb they are bare, and at passage only intercepted by a small stream of fresh water, fordable for horses.

Access to the island, which consisted of a tidal causeway, could at times be perilous; an example of how treacherous the tide could be occurred in the year 1759, when one William Thomas was sadly drowned along with his horse as he attempted the precarious journey from the island across to Cadoxton. No doubt many more people lost their lives in this way.

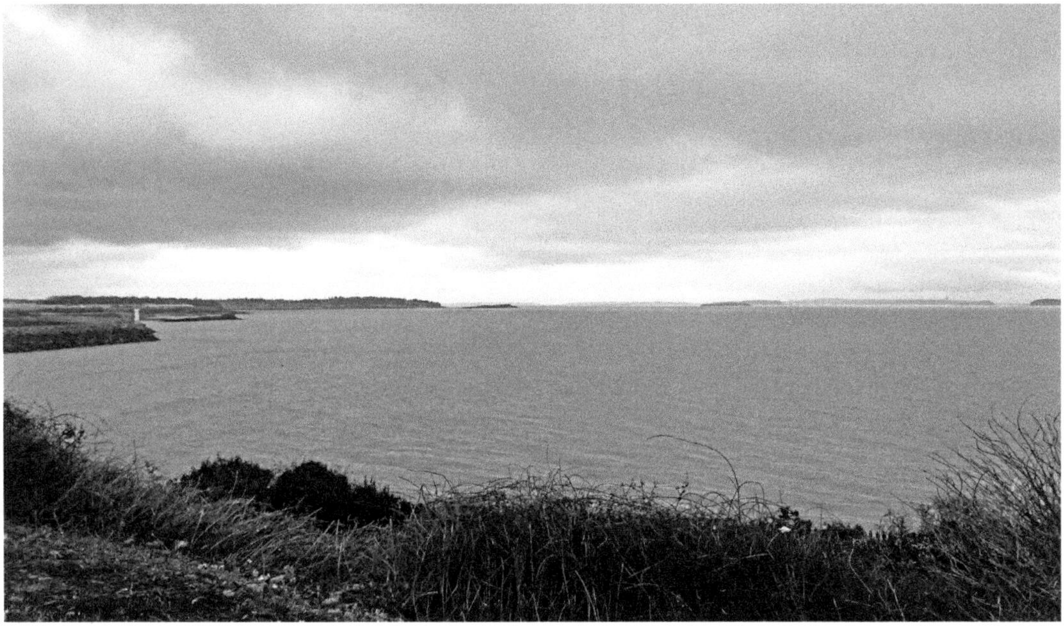

View of Sully Island from Nell's Point.

Prior to the construction of the housing and the bridge that links the island to the mainland, Barry Island, by all accounts, had always been a desolate place, with solitude being the companion of those wishing to reside there.

We can gain some impression of the island's former ambiance from a detailed account of a visit to the island written by Revd J. Evans in the year 1804, in which he narrates:

> There is no building but a farm house, fitted up as a lodging-house for those desirous of sea-bathing in retirement. And, truly, a more unmolested retreat cannot be imagined. To those that possess sufficient fortitude to brave the ennui of continual quietude, both the water and the sands are reasonable inducements. But the want of machines excludes many, especially delicate females, from enjoying the advantages arising from the situation. To us there was a characteristic dreariness, heightened by the hoarse sounding ocean, that inspired melancholy-not a tree, nor shrub, but one continued sight of sand, partially covered with short grass, which a few poor sheep were endeavouring to graze. If you ascend the hill, the wide expanding channel, and behind the well-wooded but thinly inhabited country, with the idea of being able to get off but once in twelve hours (for the boat is not properly attended to), are points that will furnish but little that is interesting to the valetudinarian or the gay. To a party, who have all their amusements amongst themselves, it may be tolerable for a time, but to those accustomed to the luxury of society and other pleasurable amusements, Barry will not furnish a single inducement to visit or reside.

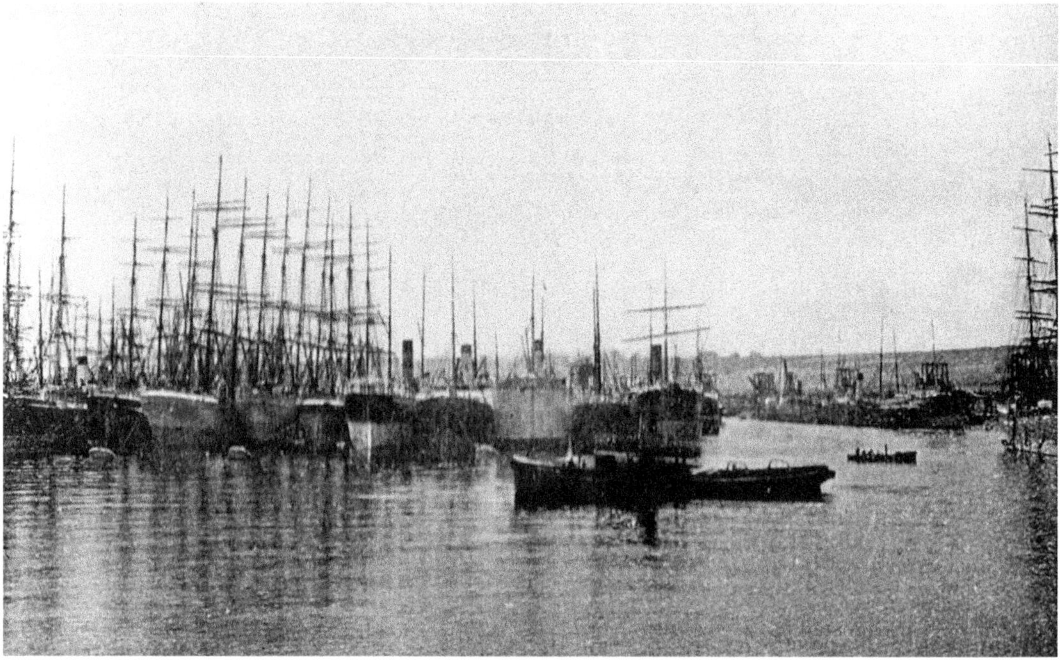

Photograph of Barry Docks during its early years. (Source: Tom Clements.)

The construction of the docks and the birth of the town of Barry during the late nineteenth century abruptly put an end to Barry Island's solitude, forever linking it to the mainland. But despite its isolation, Barry Island has been host to various communities throughout its existence and has a long and interesting history that stretches far back into antiquity, as various archaeological discoveries attest to. This book seeks, for the first time, to present the complete history of Barry Island – from the time the earliest communities settled in the Barry area, through to the late nineteenth century when the island was developed to cater for day trippers and tourists – looking at both the popular history and lesser-known history of this seaside resort.

2. Mesolithic / Neolithic

Hunter-Gatherers on Barry Island

After the end of the last Ice Age 11,500 years ago, south Wales, unlike Scotland or other parts of northern Britain, would have been wooded or covered with tundra, and the climate milder and more conducive for herds of reindeers and the bands of hunter-gatherers who followed them. It was during a broad period of the Holocene (the period after the last Ice Age, the present period) around 9600–400 BC that saw dramatic climatic changes ranging from cold, dry periods to warm, wet periods, meaning the sea levels would have gradually risen. For much of this period Barry Island would still have been joined to the mainland as a peninsula extending westwards from Sully, the sea would have been further out towards the Channel, and much of the land in the near vicinity would have been comprised of forest or tundra. In short, Barry Island would have looked very different to how it looks today.

The earliest evidence for the presence of our distant ancestors on Barry Island takes the form of flint blades dating to the Mesolithic period (10,000–4200 BC). These flint tools, or microliths, have been found on Friars Point and represent the oldest recorded archaeological finds known from Barry Island, and indeed the Barry area at large. These microliths would have been used as arrowheads or spear points, which were used by our ancient ancestors for hunting a variety of animals including pig, red deer, elk and wild cattle, but would also have been used to spear fish.

The people living in Wales during the Mesolithic period are thought to have been predominantly hunter-gatherers who usually didn't stay in one place for any great length of time, although they did seem to prefer to confine their activities to or near coastal areas. Certainly one of Wales's most well-known Mesolithic sites, located at Goldcliff near Newport (approximately 30 miles away) and dating to 6000–4700 BC, seems to confirm this and represents a microcosm of Mesolithic activity, with many interesting finds of note being discovered, including scatters of flint such as those found on Barry Island, remains of foodstuff, and interestingly, human footprints including those of children. Occupation of this unique archaeological site is thought to have been on a seasonal basis, in particular during the summer and autumn months. It is possible that Barry Island, much like Goldcliff, could also have been occupied on a seasonal basis during the Mesolithic period.

A polished Neolithic Celt or stone axe head, uncovered by Mr John Conybeare while out walking during the nineteenth century, represents the next significant prehistoric discovery on Barry Island. Another more complete example of the same type of implement was found during the construction of the docks. Neolithic artefacts have also been discovered in the area surrounding Barry. A stone axe dating from the Neolithic period was discovered nearby in the parish of St Andrew's; this find complements

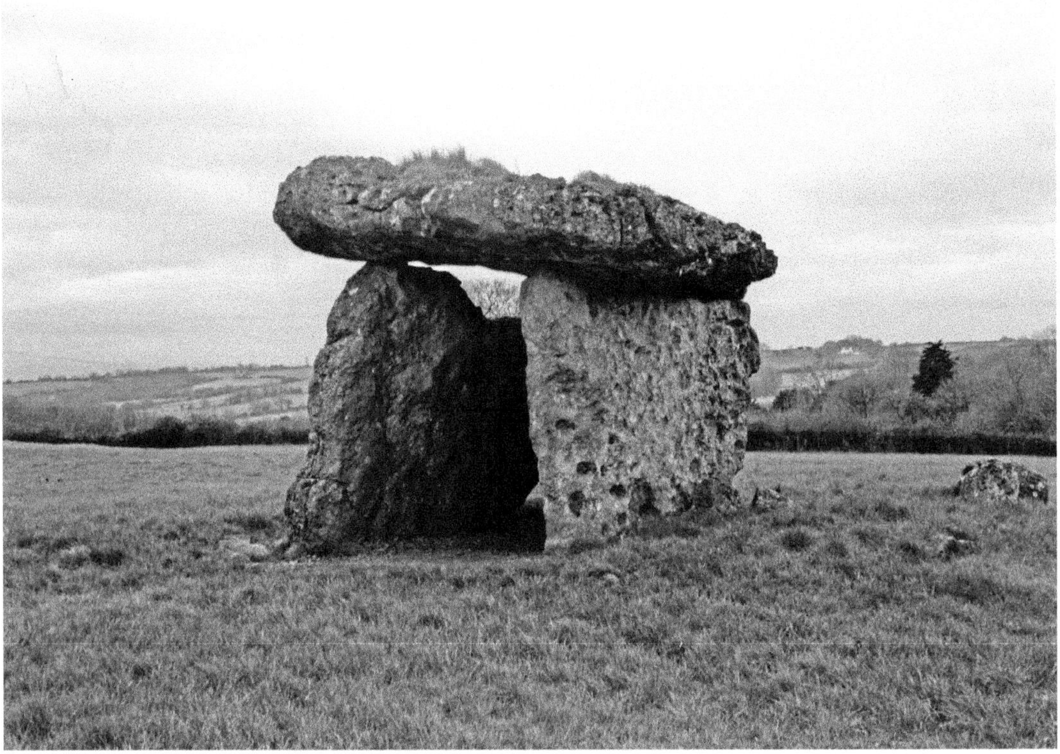

St Lythans Neolithic tomb.

another similar Neolithic axe found within the same area in 1920s, testifying that Barry Island was a part of a larger Neolithic community.

The Neolithic period (4200–2500 BC) saw a gradual cessation of the mobile hunter-gatherer lifestyle to a more sedentary existence involving the cultivation of crops, animal husbandry, and construction of both domestic buildings and monumental architecture. It was during the Neolithic period that we begin to see the construction of tombs such as the megalithic burial chambers at nearby St Lythans and Tinkinswood. We also see the introduction of pottery and a new variety of stone implements – such as the polished stone axe head found on Barry Island – in more widespread use.

Until fairly recently Barry Island possessed a number of prehistoric burial chambers that were extant on Friars Point, suggesting some sort of community living in the near vicinity. Certainly, there are similar chambers or barrows scattered throughout the Barry area, with two examples formerly existing at nearby Cold Knap, both of which have been destroyed by erosion or the Atlantic Trading Estate. There is also another located in the west end of Barry, the aptly named 'Westward Corner Barrow'. These prehistoric barrows date to the Bronze Age.

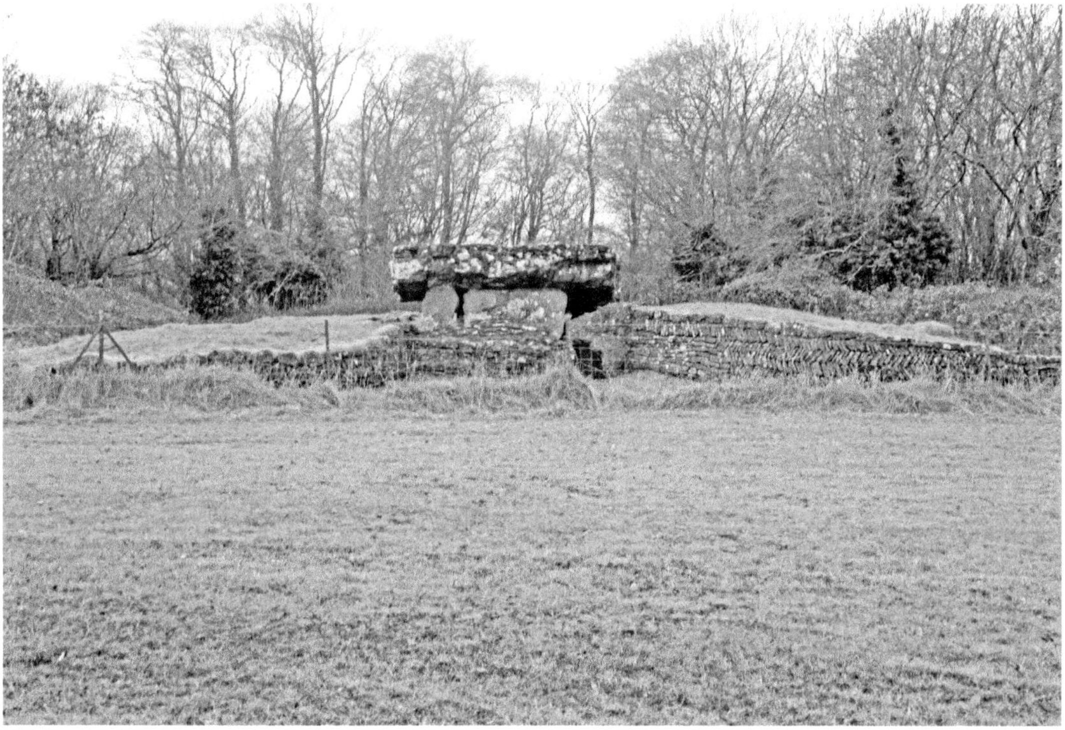

Tinkinswood Neolithic tomb.

3. Bronze Age Barry Island

Burials, Barrows, and Departure from the Mainland

Burials contained within barrows from the Bronze Age (2500–800 BC) are usually in marked contrast to those found in earlier Neolithic barrows such as those excavated at Tinkinswood and St Lythans, and other Cotswold-Severn variety tombs, which tend to contain multiple internments. Barrows dating to the Bronze Age mostly tend to contain single burials. These ancient and enigmatic monuments are thought to be more than simply a place to bury the deceased, and arc not only associated with ancestor veneration but were also used as a form of territorial marker to denote boundaries.

Theoretically, it has been postulated that these types of burials were generally reserved for an elite; this is based on their relative disparity in regard to an assumed larger population. Although impossible to verify, the authors believe this highly probable – are we really to believe that there were just six people living in or around Friars Point during the whole Bronze Age? The elite paradigm seems more likely, with some archaeologists even suggesting that the occupants of such graves could be related. Therefore, during prehistory Friars Point was most likely a cemetery for a forgotten and obscure elite.

It was at some point during the Bronze Age that the peninsula extending westward from Sully became separated from the mainland, creating Barry Island, but, despite its departure from the mainland, during the Bronze Age Barry Island was connected to a wider community, as the Vale of Glamorgan contains an abundance of Bronze Age archaeological sites. For example, although rare, archaeologists are occasionally lucky enough to find a settlement with evidence for actual occupation, such as the enigmatic ditched enclosure and midden site recently excavated at Llanmaes. This

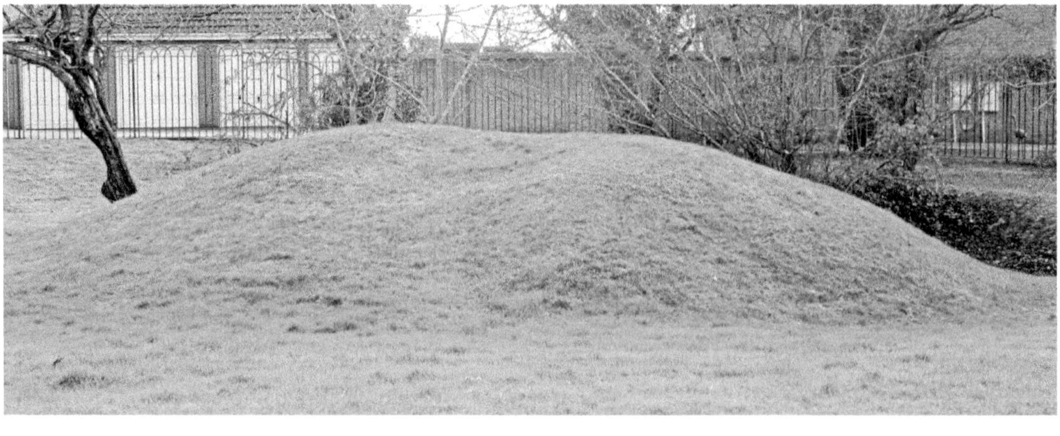

Westward Corner barrow, which dates to the mid- to late Bronze Age.

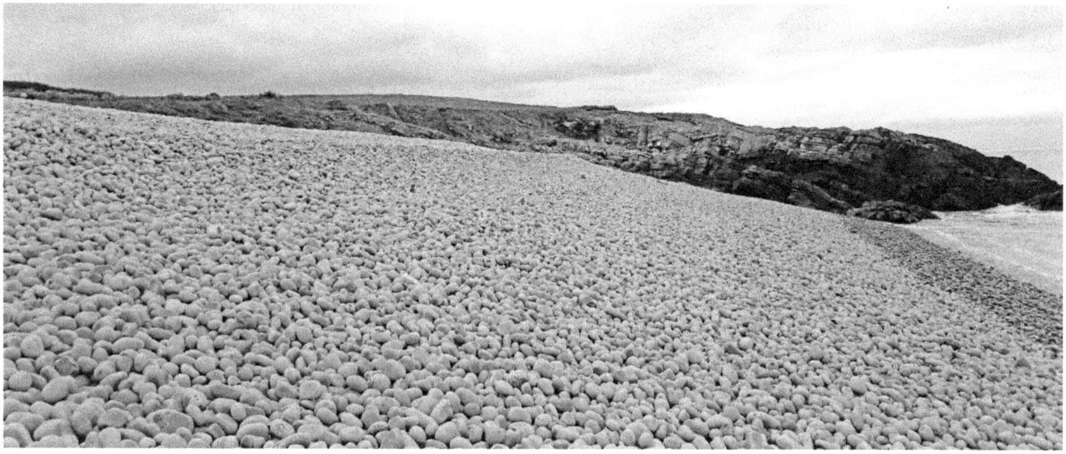

The Knap location of the now vanished Bronze Age barrow.

dates to the middle Bronze Age, with activity spanning into the Iron Age and Roman periods. Occupation of the Llanmaes site for the most part seems to have taken the form of some sort of ritualised and communal feasting within the enclosure itself, with people travelling from both the locality and from great distances to take part. It is almost certain that people living in the Barry Island area would have visited such an eminent location.

The barrows found on Friars Point, like those found in the near vicinity, are single round mounds, and although a number of them were confirmed to date from the Bronze Age, some, due to the paucity of datable evidence, are of a less certain lineage. There was once a total of six of these curious round earthen lumps noted on Friars Point. These ancient and enigmatic curiosities were among the first archaeological features on Barry Island to attract the attention of antiquarians, who subjected them to various archaeological excavations during the late nineteenth century. Due to the repeated attentions of Victorian archaeologists, however, we are now left with very little left to observe in the present day.

DID YOU KNOW?

Three of the Bronze Age barrows on Friars Point were in fact excavated twice, by two different individuals, first by John Romilly Allen in 1872 and again by John Storrie in 1894.

Barrow-digging antiquarian style was very much a gentleman's hobby during the eighteenth and nineteenth centuries. Often rich landowners with vast estates such as Richard Colt Hoare (1758–1838) would subject any curiosities on their land to rough and

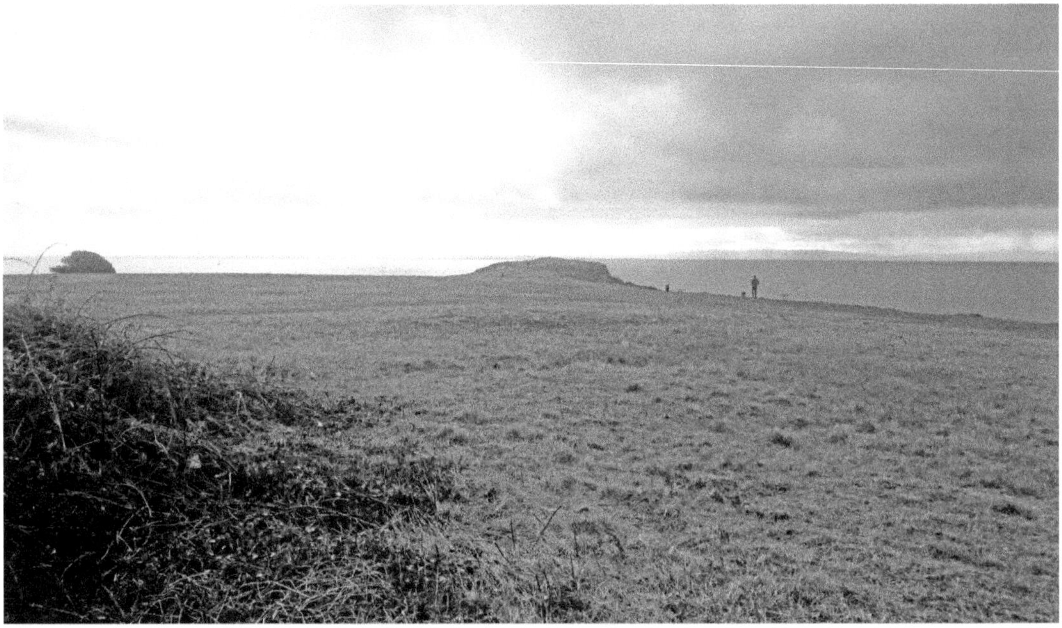

Friars Point facing south and the majority of the barrows.

brutal excavations, with little or no thought given to anything outside the pursuit of finding treasures to fill their mantelpieces, and in the process destroying much valuable evidence – although these activities did lay the basis for modern archaeology. John Romilly Allen, an engineer and archaeologist, subjected these mounds to their first responsible, if not slightly haphazard, excavations in 1872. However, the irresponsible actions of unknown barrow diggers prior to Romilly's excavations unfortunately rendered the subsequent interpretations of a number of the tumuli skewed and incomplete, although in a few instances enough dating material was left to deduce age and archaeological character of the mounds. Romilly excavated three mounds in total during 1872. Surveying the scene before him, Romilly summarised what he saw as, 'on the extreme end of this promontory will be found three rude mounds.' Full of Victorian zeal, he went to work with alacrity.

Following the previous explorations of John Romilly Allen, archaeologist John Storrie was commissioned in 1894 by Barry Island's then owner Lord Windsor to investigate any potential archaeological features on Friars Point. This saw him not only re-examining the mounds excavated by Romilly, but also excavating three other mounds missed by Romilly. In fact, Storrie counted six mounds instead of the three Romilly observed.

A mound located furthest south towards the tip of Friars Point was the first to be excavated by Romilly in 1872 and was subsequently reopened by Storrie in 1894. This mound was described by Romilly as 'the largest of the group of three' he excavated that year; his interventions were minimal, though, as he noted that it had already been previously disturbed. Romilly stated that its contents had, at least in part, been removed to make a beacon and thus he took no further action; his results here were therefore inconclusive.

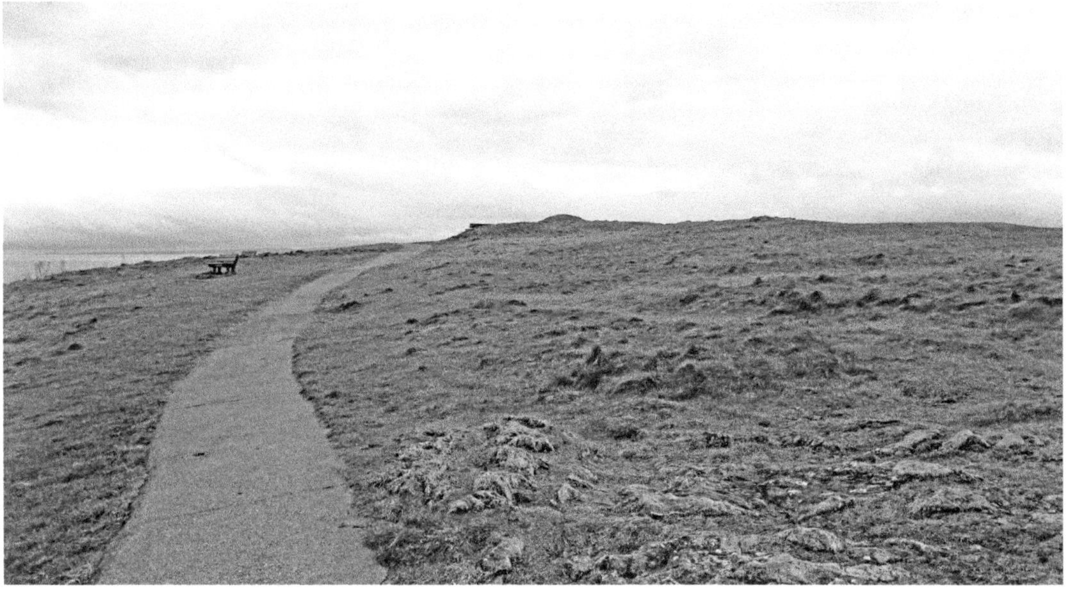

View of the apex of Friars Point.

By the time Storrie arrived to re-examine this mound in 1894 there was little left for him to record or excavate, describing the mound as having 'been completely dug out'. It was noted by Storrie that even the very stones the mound was composed of had been removed and used in the construction of a flagstaff mound, hence any archaeological information, if ever there was any, would have been permanently lost.

The mound, described in its location as being 'the middle one', proved somewhat of a disappointment to Romilly, describing its contents as 'debris of shells and some argillaceous soil mixed with stones'. It is possible that, with the advancement of theoretical thought connected with the study of Bronze Age funerary monuments and practices, to suggest that what John Romilly Allen happened across may have been a form of midden (a rubbish dump), perhaps with ritual symbolic connotations connected with forgotten and obscure funerary rites, such as we see within the burial chambers of Neolithic long barrows. Perhaps in a Victorian-like craving for treasure and wonderful artefacts, Romilly held no regard for assemblages or items not of a collectable nature.

This mound's seeming lack of prehistoric credentials didn't deter John Storrie from re-excavating it in 1894. During this time the mound, despite having been previously excavated, still measured 6.9 metres in diameter. Storrie wasted no time in cutting a trench across the mound, which was 9.1 metres long by 1.5 metres wide. He got to the natural geology beneath where he found the charred remains of a human being that had been cremated and then covered with a thin slab of limestone; a human tooth and fragments of cranium were among the tangible remains available for study. Storrie even records there being a secondary burial in this mound, possibly skeletal remains, although unfortunately over the many centuries of its interment it had been disturbed

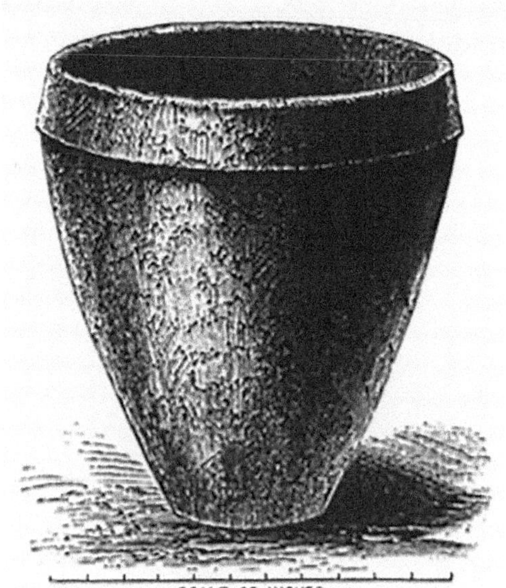

The Bronze Age urn drawn by John Romilly Allen. (Source: Cambrian Archaeological Society.)

by animals leaving almost no physical trace of its remains. Subsequent analysis of the scant remains by the National Museum of Wales Department of Zoology were mostly inconclusive, other than confirming the remains were human, although this was before the advent of radiocarbon dating, which can provide firm date ranges for ancient organic remains.

The final mound, excavated in the summer of 1872, was also the smallest according to Romilly and his younger brothers, who pitched in with the excavations. It measured 3 metres in diameter and with what Romilly describes as an apex of some 0.9 metres. It was noted by Romilly as being composed of earth, clay, stones and shells. Romilly also observed that the construction of this mound was similar to the centre mound he excavated on Friars Point, which might suggest a contemporary relationship between the two monuments. Romilly decided to cut a trench through the mound. During this investigation he happened across an archaic burial in the form of cremated bones; in this instance they were contained within an ancient vessel, what Romilly describes as an urn that was 'of roughly baked clay, inverted on a flat stone'. This urn was later identified as being of a middle Bronze Age type that belonged to a time when there was a marked shift in Bronze Age burial practices from inhumation to cremation. Unfortunately, despite Romilly's protestations about being careful, he managed to break the urn during its removal, saying, 'it was found impossible to get it out whole' – the urn is now with the National Museum of Wales. Despite having conclusive evidence of its antiquity, Romilly expressed his disappointment at not finding anything else of note in this barrow.

According to Storrie, not long after Romilly had made his intrusions into this mound, it was visited by a Mr J. W. Lukis, who apparently 'saw the remains of

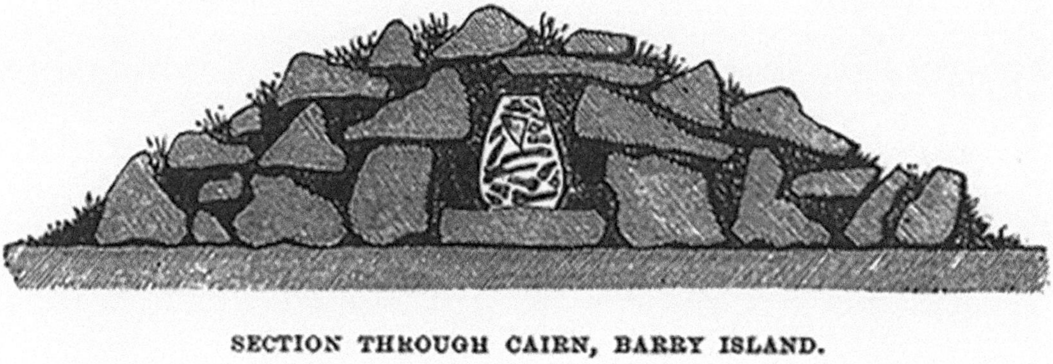

Victorian drawing of the urn mound by John Romilly Allen. (Source: Cambrian Archaeological Society.)

three separate interments encircled by sea shells and small stones'. The details of this, however, are somewhat vague and it is unclear if he means full interments or cremations. Storrie conducted his own excavation of the mound in 1895 and, although the mound is undoubtedly of great antiquity, being a bona fide example of a Bronze Age round barrow, Storrie found only the contents of a midden, namely the remains of foodstuffs such as shells, limpets and winkles, as well as a few flints and a solitary fragment of pottery. It was also noted that the site was on top of the remains of a large fire. This mound was still visible in the 1930s when Aileen Fox took an interest in these barrows.

Despite playing second fiddle on re-excavating three of the mounds due to the earlier work of Romilly, John Storrie did have the sole monopoly of excavating the remaining three mounds. The first of the mounds Storrie excavated by himself was located on the eastern side of Friars Point, near the now vanished Treharne's Pier. Storrie put a 10-metres by 1.8-metres-wide trench in and found only a cut feature, a trench that circled the mound; the trench was described as being 15.2 metres all around. No finds of substance were found, suggesting that this mound was perhaps of no great antiquity.

Another barrow was opened by Storrie in 1894, having been previously ignored by Romilly. Storrie noted it was roughly 3 metres in diameter and was located in the extreme south-east corner of Friars Point. Storrie put a trench through this mound 'down to the living rock', but he found very little, describing its contents as 'a few particles of charcoal intermixed with soil and stones'. This is hardly surprising as Storrie himself says of the mound that 'all appearances showed it had been opened at no distant date', and by the 1930s there was no visible trace of it left at all.

The final barrow to be excavated by Storrie resembled what he described as a 'large tumulus', which had unfortunately been opened prior to systematic excavation. As thorough as Storrie's excavations were, very few finds of note were made. Storrie may have jumped to conclusions when he asserted that 'all traces of burial removed', although it is possible this mound once contained human remains. It was later postulated by Aileen Fox that this could have been a pillow mound due to the mound's large circumference and external ditch, deliberately dug as a rabbit warren and, hence, not dating from prehistory.

DID YOU KNOW?

John Storrie happened across a mysterious stone cist while excavations were commencing on the harbour pier close to Friars Point in 1895. Inside were the remains of a female in the form of a crouched skeleton. John Storrie placed the cist within the remains of St Baruc's Chapel, where they still reside today.

With the end of the Bronze Age came the Iron Age (800–43 BC). Later Iron Age settlements are well represented in the locality, such as the Bulwarks promontory near Porthkerry, Westward Corner Iron Age settlement and the Iron Age/Romano-British farmstead at Whitton located along the Five Mile Lane, showing a thriving local community. Sadly there are no known archaeological remains dating to the Iron Age on Barry Island, although it is not unreasonable to assume that there was some sort of occupation of Barry Island during this period.

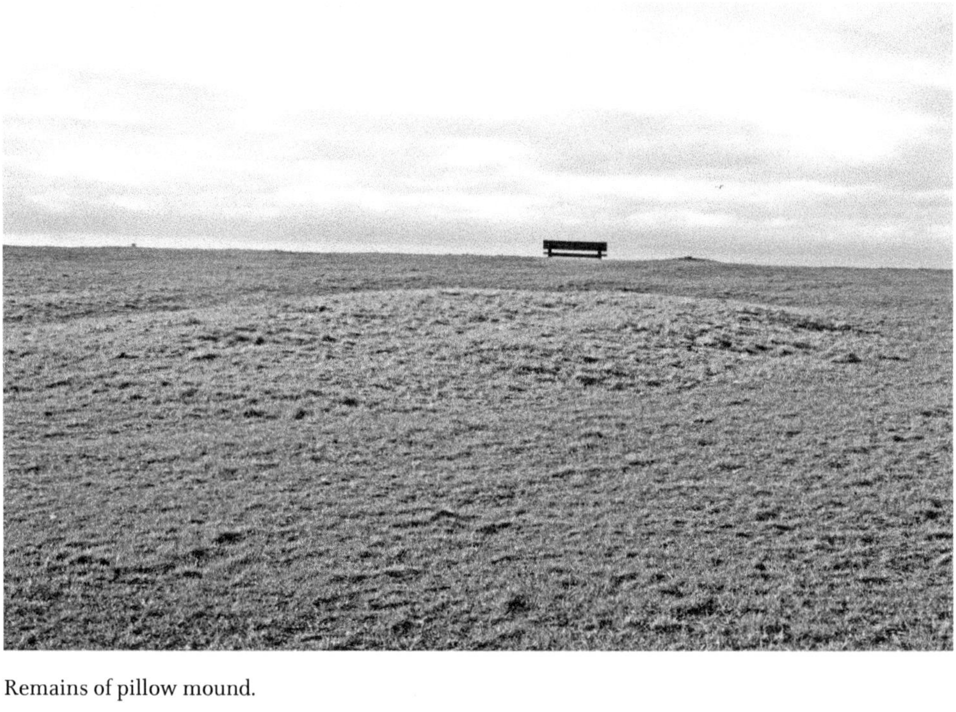

Remains of pillow mound.

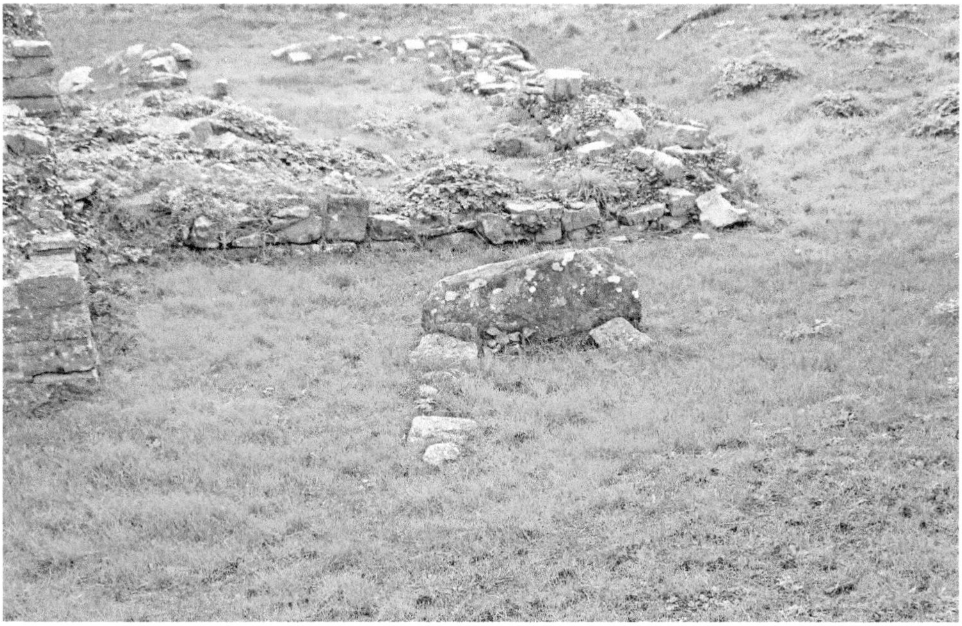

A stone cist that held the remains of a female burial.

4. Romano-British Period

Roman Presence

The influence of the Roman Empire in Britain was considerable; for nearly four centuries, the cultural and political authority of Rome was prevalent throughout Britain. Despite being in one of the most remote, far-flung corners of the Roman Empire, south Wales was certainly very much under Rome's control. This influence, which is represented in everything from architecture to burial practice, and particularly material culture, is reflected in the archaeology of the region, which exists in proliferation.

Roman influence in south Wales began with the construction of a series of forts at Cardiff, the earliest of which dates to the middle of the first century AD. The

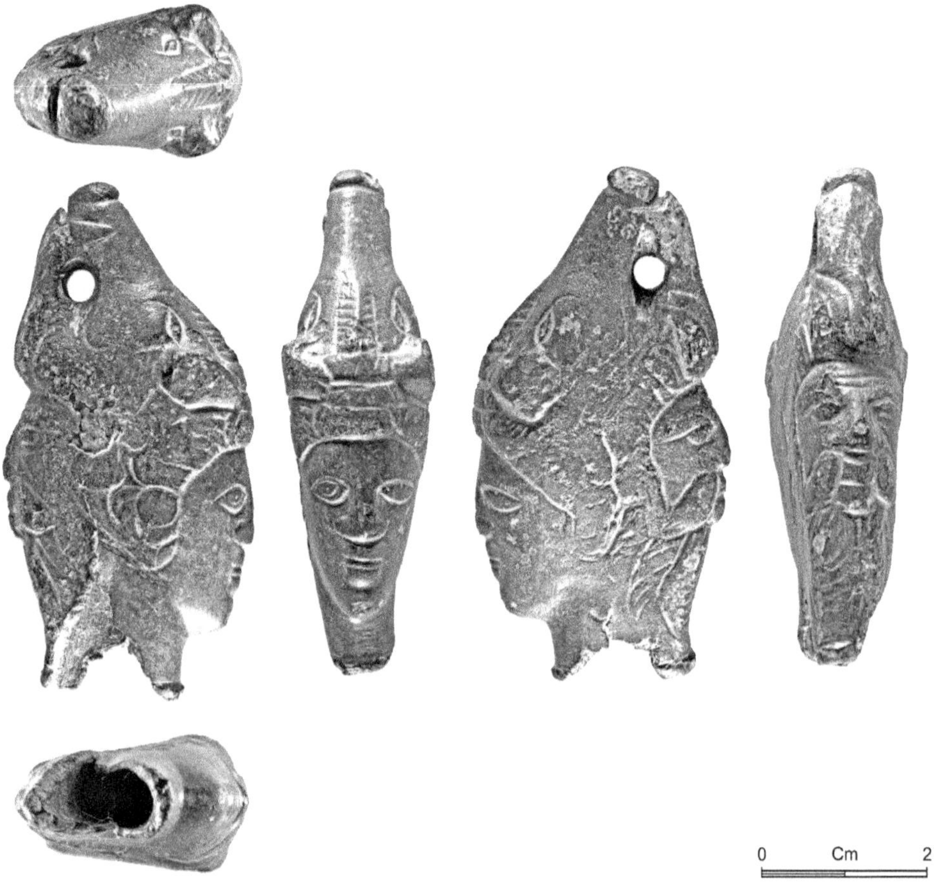

Roman key handle found in the Barry area. (Source: Portable Antiquities Scheme Wales.)

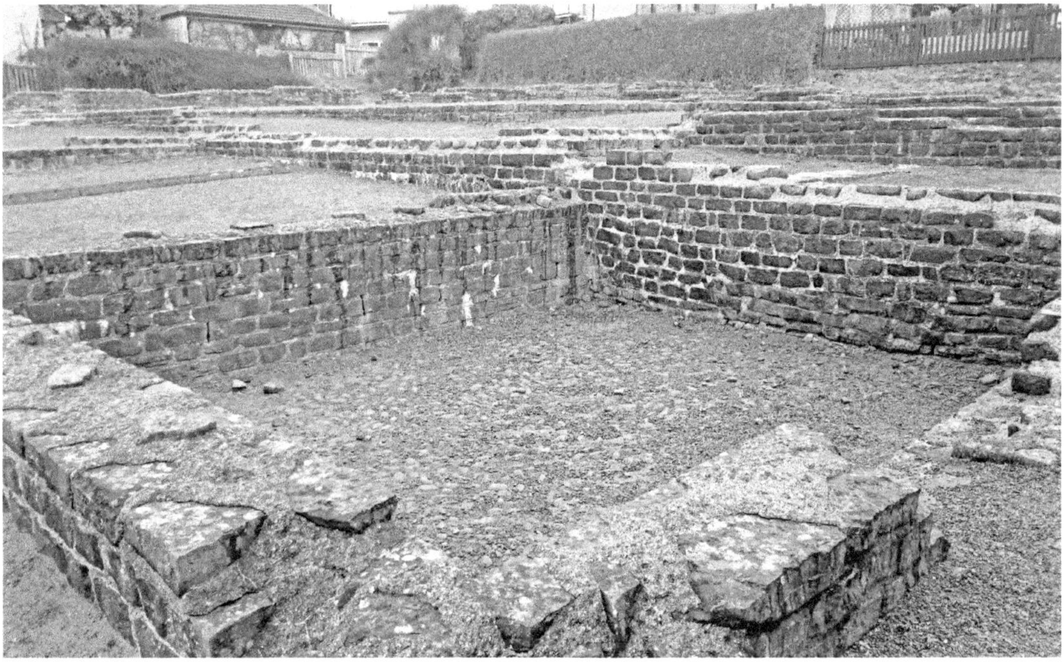

Roman building at Glan-y-Mor.

presence of the Roman military at Cardiff provided the impetus for Roman influence to permeate south Wales and beyond. The area around Barry has been shown through archaeology to have been extensively Romanised. For example, at Glan-y-Mor near Cold Knap there are the remains of a twenty-two-roomed villa-like structure dating to the third or fourth century AD. A lack of refinements such as a hypocaust system suggests a utilitarian purpose for this structure, perhaps connected with the military. There are excavated Iron Age/Romano-British period farmsteads at Biglis and Whitton, as well as on Dinas Powys common and a settlement located at nearby Pop Hill. In addition there is an Iron Age/Romano-British hill fort at the Bulwarks near Porthkerry, and no less than two large Roman period coin hoards have been unearthed at Sully.

Given the extensive Romanisation of the surrounding area, it is of little surprise that Roman artefacts have been discovered on Barry Island. John Storrie uncovered various Roman artefacts on the island during the late nineteenth century, indicating a Roman presence in the vicinity. During Storrie's St Barruc's Chapel excavations, for example, Storrie found Roman tiles and a Roman brick built into the wall of one of the chapel's associated buildings. This occurrence, however, provides no certainty of a bona fide Romano-British period building on the island as it was fairly common for people to reuse Roman period building material during the centuries after the Roman Empire withdrew from Britain.

The various Roman period buildings that dotted the landscape provided a cheap and readily available source of dressed stone and other materials of use. We see good examples of this occurrence at Old Barry Village, where reused Roman material was incorporated into some of the medieval period peasant houses, and also the contemporary priest's house adjacent to St Nicholas' Church – thus it is most likely the Roman brick and tiles were simply taken from elsewhere and built into the later period structure, with the Roman building at Cold Knap being a likely source.

Storrie also found several Roman coins in the near vicinity of St Barruc's Chapel. These finds, however, were not found in a proper archaeological context and were essentially un-stratified, meaning that they must unfortunately be regarded as casual losses not associated with any structure or settlement. Storrie was even of the opinion that one of the Roman coins – a silver denarius of Julia Mammae – he found near the chapel of St Barruc was planted there at a recent date, in his own words to 'purposely hoax' him.

DID YOU KNOW?

John Storrie excavated two mounds on Friars Road, which he termed 'British Kitchen' – he attributed these archaeological features to the Iron Age Romano-British period. These mounds revealed the shells of oysters, limpets and periwinkles, as well as variety of fish and animal bones, flint flakes and pottery. Subsequent analysis of these finds, however, have revealed that this particular feature was most likely a midden/cooking area dating from the twelfth to thirteenth centuries.

Storrie also uncovered what he termed a 'Roman well', located at the intersection of Harbour Road and Station Approach Road close to the railway embankment. Storrie was perhaps too credulous in ascribing Roman antecedents to the well, as the only Roman find associated with this structure was a first- to second-century Roman fibula (brooch) that was found nearby to the south of the well, with the only find from inside the well comprising of a small copper pendant dating to the medieval period. The close proximity of the well to medieval archaeology and general lack of Roman period evidence strongly suggests that the well, in all likelihood, dates to the medieval period.

Despite the fact that various Roman artefacts have been discovered on Barry Island, conclusive evidence for Romano-British period structures is sadly lacking. Certainly people living in the Barry area during the Romano-British period came to Barry Island, as the discovery of Roman coins and artefacts attest to, and perhaps even constructed buildings here, but at present the Roman finds from Barry Island can do little more than hint at an established community of some sort in the near vicinity.

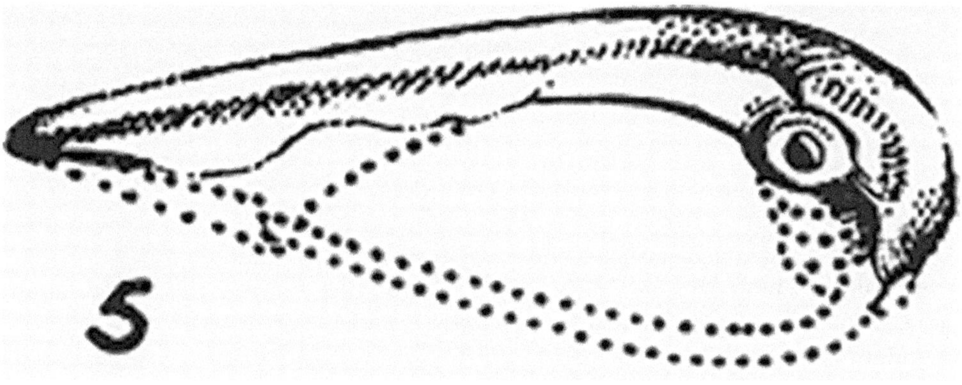

Roman brooch from the Paget Road and Station Road area. (Source: Cardiff Naturalists Society.)

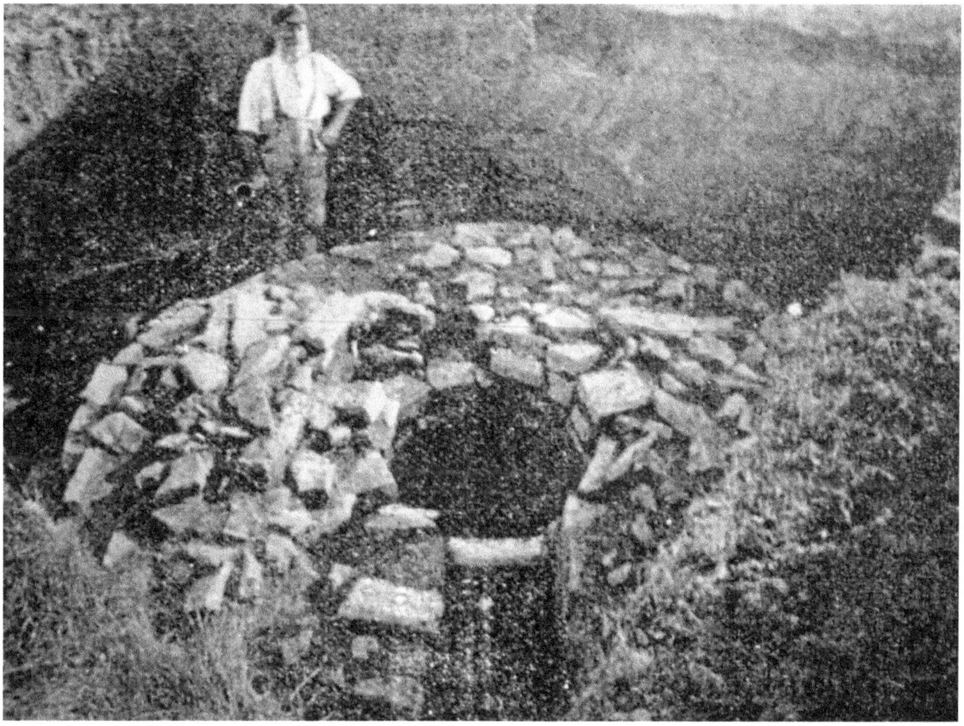

'Roman' well area before modern construction engulfed it. (Source: Cardiff Naturalists Society.)

5. Early Medieval Period

A Dark Period?

Rome officially withdrew from Britain during the early fifth century, taking with it its social, political and cultural influence. It seems society collapsed almost overnight as archaeologically there is not a great deal of evidence to suggest that the communities that existed during the Romano-British period survived into the early medieval period in south Wales. Certainly the farmsteads at nearby Whitton, Biglis, Dinas Powys and the settlement at Pop Hill, some of which were almost continually occupied throughout the Romano-British period, show no evidence of occupation after Rome left Britain to fend for itself. However, the presence of two early Christian cemeteries located at nearby Atlantic Trading Estate and Llandough respectively, and the possible reoccupation of the Roman villa-like building at Glan-y-Mor during the centuries after Roman occupation ended, shows that civilisation had not been entirely extinguished in the Glamorgan area.

This was, however, truly a 'dark' period of the history of not just the Vale of Glamorgan but the whole of Wales. One can almost imagine a wasteland of uncultivated fields with neglected Roman field systems, crumbing Roman villas and structures, disregarded since their builders left these shores. After generations of reverting to scratching a living in prehistoric-style wood and thatch huts (such as the Grubenhaus in Saxon England), the inhabitants of Wales simply lost the skills required to even maintain the sophisticated Roman structures, the ruins of which were still standing into the high medieval period, whereas in some places, such as at Glan-y-Mor at Barry, they were known enough to be robbed of their stone.

The early medieval period was a time of monks, monasteries and hermits. Christianity slowly permeated through the British Isles, from the halls of Saxon kings through to the most remote and lonely parts of Britain and Ireland – an omnipresent force that deeply affected the communities that succumbed to its teachings. Despite its tiny population, the early medieval period in Glamorgan was a time when the fledgling religion of Christianity flourished. Certainly Glamorgan had its share of religious establishments during this period, with the monasteries at Llantwit Major and Llancarfan both being important centres of early Christian learning.

During the early medieval period Barry Island was home to a Christian shrine, which was dedicated to St Barruc. The origins of the man whose name was given to the island, village and consequently the town are obscure. The earliest written reference to St Barruc was written by Lifris of Llancarfan in *Vita Sancti Cadoci*, which dates to around 1100 and tells us the story connecting St Barruc with Barry Island. It is likely that this account had been in existence for quite some time before Lifris committed it to paper, and was almost certainly based on earlier written material and oral tradition.

> The Blessed Codoc [St Cadoc] at a certain day sailed with two of his disciples named Barruc and Gwalches from the island of Echni [Flat Holm] to another Island named

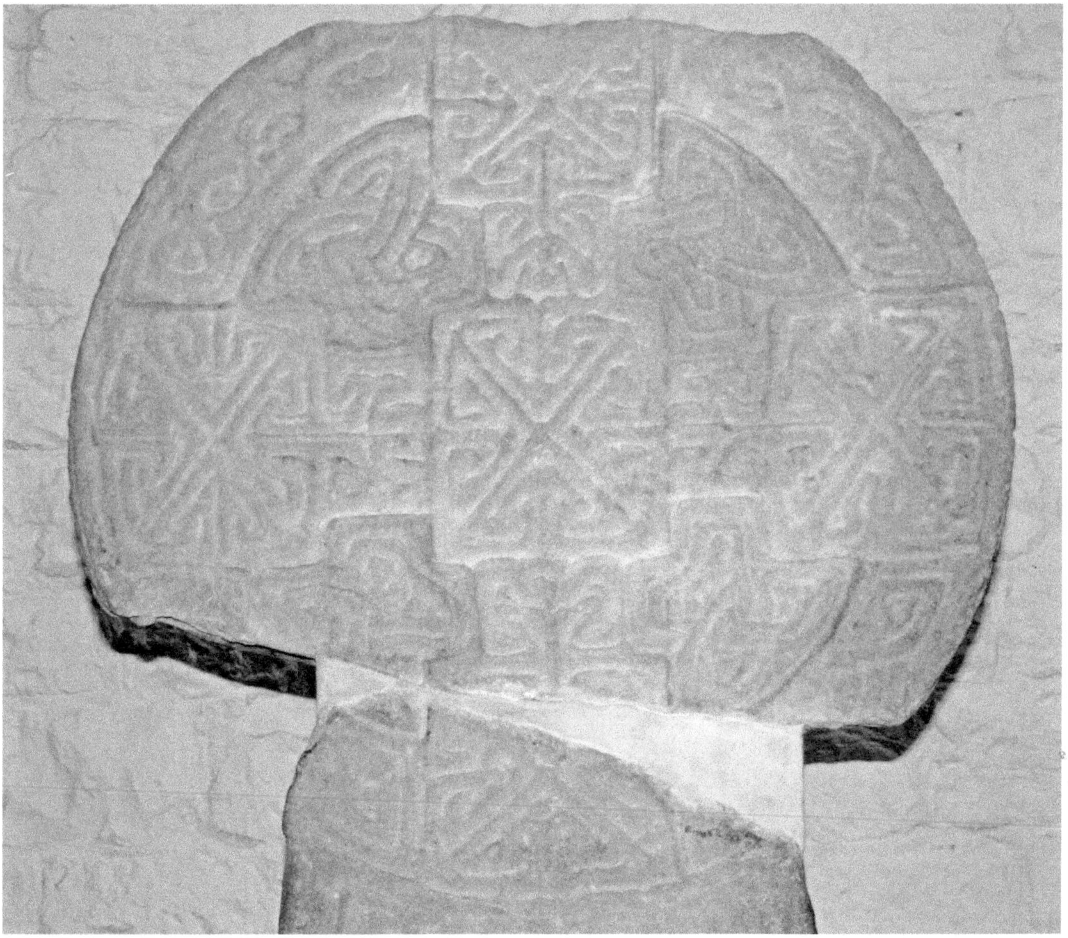

Celtic/Christian religious cross from Llantwit Major.

> Barren [Barry]. When, therefore, he prosperously landed at the harbour, he asked his said disciples for his Enchiridion, that is, manual book, and they confessed that they had, through forgetfulness, left it at the aforesaid island, which hearing, he immediately compelled them to go aboard the ship and sail back to recover the book, and burning with anger, said 'go not return!'.

It seems that Cadoc got his wish, for the story narrates that the two disciples went back to the island to fetch the book, and were both drowned on their return. Gwalches was buried on Flat Holm while Barruc was buried on Barry Island. Whether this version of events actually happened or not is certainly open to debate, but what we can be certain of is that sometime after the alleged event a shrine dedicated to St Barruc was erected on Barry Island, culminating with the construction of a stone chapel during the medieval period.

It is impossible to give a definitive date to the site of St Barruc's shrine as a place of pilgrimage, but what would have existed before the construction of the first stone chapel would most likely have been an open-air shrine. The exact location of this early shrine is unknown, but it's likely that the area around it was being used as a cemetery for some time before the first stone chapel was constructed.

DID YOU KNOW?

During the early medieval period, Barry Island, for a time, appears to have been host to a fleet of Orkney Vikings. *The Life of St Gwynllyw of Newport* tells us that these Vikings, who were apparently under the pay of Gruffydd ap Llywelyn, ravaged much of south Wales in the year 1049. The early Christian monasteries and centres of learning in Llancarfan and Llantwit Major would have provided sufficient inducement to attract a Viking raiding party to south Wales; both Llantwit Major and Llancarfan suffered Viking raids in 988.

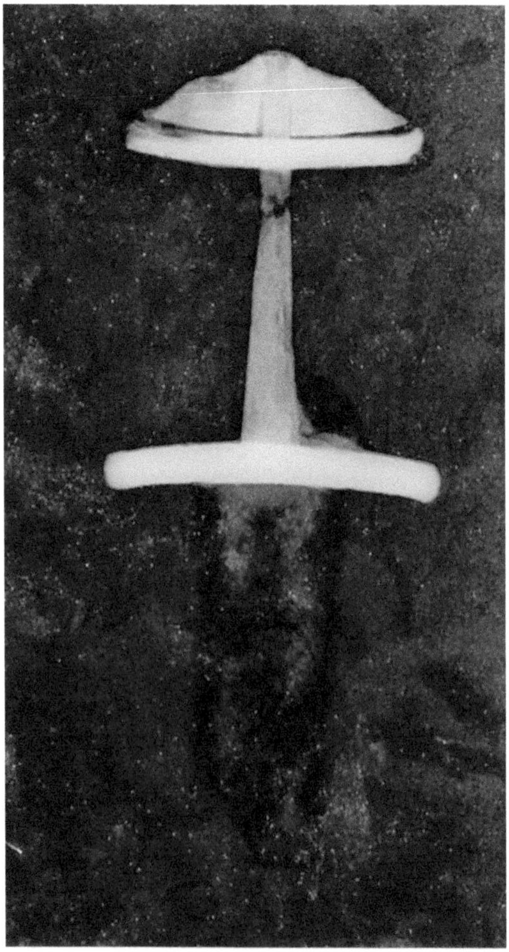

Viking sword found within the Vale of Glamorgan. (Source: Portable Antiquities Scheme Wales.)

6. Medieval Period

Saints, Sand and Pilgrims

During the medieval period a small chapel was constructed on Barry Island dedicated to St Barruc. The chapel was in use from the twelfth century to the sixteenth century, when its popularity gradually diminished and it fell into decay and disrepair; it had disappeared entirely by the time Revd J. Evans visited the island in 1804.

The chapel of St Barruc would have fulfilled a number of purposes during its existence, such as administering the rites of baptism, marriage and burial. St Barruc's Chapel's primary function, however, appears to have been to house the enshrined remains of St Barruc, which attracted many pilgrims throughout its existence and brought in much-needed revenue for the chapel's upkeep.

What could a pilgrim hope to gain out of their visit to St Barruc's Chapel? In our secular and materialistic twenty-first-century world, it is difficult for many people to comprehend the importance that religion played in the lives of our ancestors. Religion was an omnipresent force that was taken seriously by all ranks of society – from kings to the lowest-born serf. It provided the individual with a set of beliefs that governed every aspect of their day-to-day lives and, depending on how well they adhered to these beliefs, their fate during the next. The medieval world was one of saints, miracles and visions. In an age where medicine was primitive, most people did not live beyond the age of thirty. Disease and death were never very far away and so spiritual health was considered just as important, if not more important, than bodily health.

An individual, therefore, might visit a religious shrine such as St Barruc's in search of a cure for a particular illness. Indeed, St Barruc's Well, located on Nell's Point near to St Barruc's Chapel, was noted by local leaseholder David Spencer, who visited Barry Island during the late seventeenth century, as 'a well of very good water wch cures ye King's evill (scrofula) , fevers, agues and is good for pains in ye head and for sores eyes'. It was widely believed that such wells and the water therein contained curative properties, and that depositing an offering into a holy or sacred well would induce the associated deity – in this case St Barruc – to bestow his blessing upon the individual concerned.

Another reason to pay a visit to a religious shrine was to appeal for remission of earthly sin, with the individual paying a (usually small) fee for access to sacred relics. These relics could consist of the bones of a particular saint, the remains of their coffin or articles that were associated with the saint during their life; in the superstitious world of medieval Christianity, these were also thought to possess curative properties.

The present remains of St Barruc's Chapel date, for the most part, to the early fourteenth century and consist of little more than a series of low standing stone walls; it certainly takes a leap of imagination to visualise the 'fair litle chapel' that Leland spoke of when he visited Barry Island during the sixteenth century. Archaeology, however, has revealed

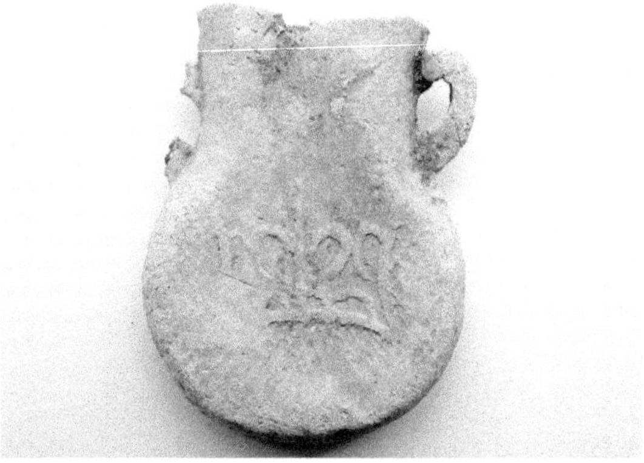

Late medieval pilgrim's ampulla found near Barry. (Source: Author's collection.)

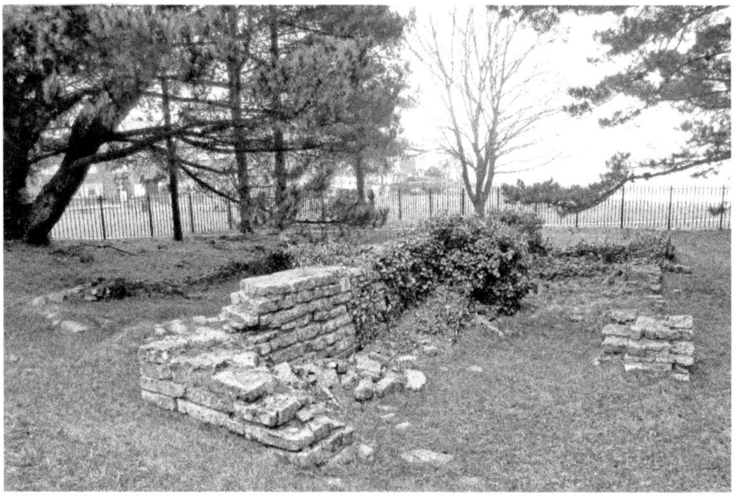

View of St Barruc's Chapel.

many of the chapel's internal and external features and has helped us to gain a greater understanding of the functions that the chapel of St Barruc administered.

John Storrie led the first series of excavations at St Barruc's Chapel – once again at the request of the island's then owner, Lord Windsor. This proved to be a sage decision as it did not take long for Storrie to uncover the remains of antiquity. Storrie at first chanced upon several burials when sewer trenches were being dug on the newly constructed Friars Road, contiguous to which were a series of sand-covered mounds, some of which were several feet high. These mounds were promptly excavated and proved to be the remains of St Barruc's Chapel. The excavations carried out by John Storrie and his team were conducted during the summers of 1894–95 and not only uncovered the remains of St Barruc's Chapel and associated buildings but also evidence of a cemetery, which Storrie claimed contained thousands of bodies. However, this claim may very well be exaggerated, or a leap of faith at best, as without the aid of modern archaeological science such as geophysics it would have been almost impossible for Storrie to know this unless he actually physically excavated thousands of bodies.

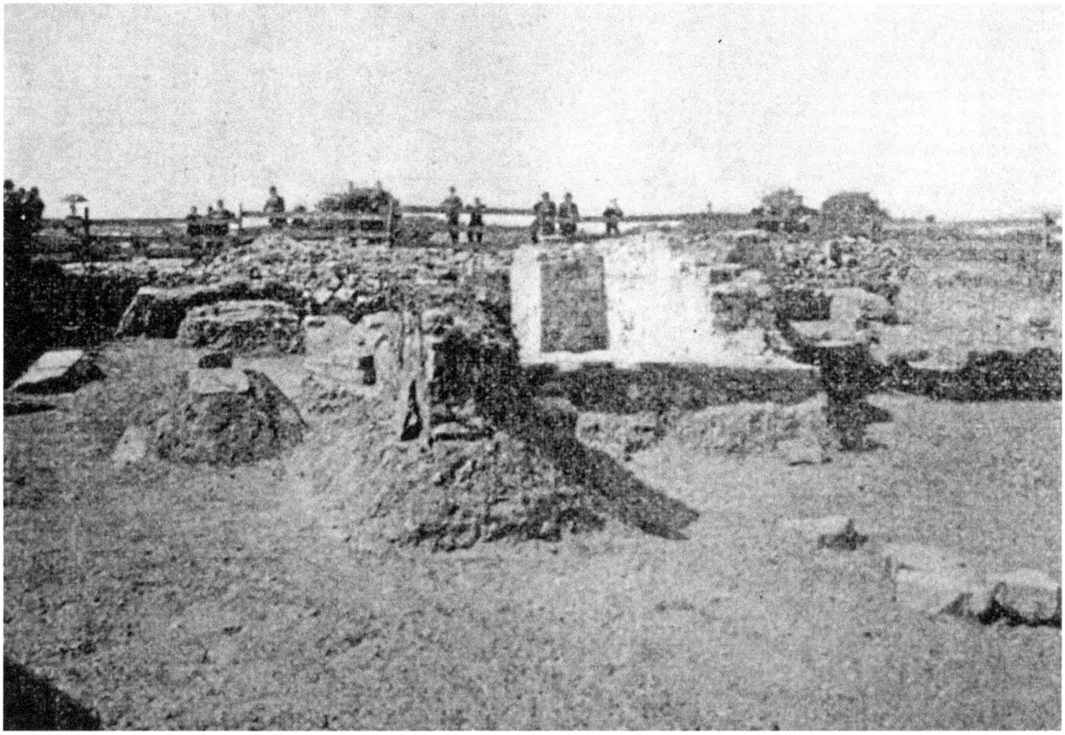

Photograph of St Barruc's Chapel when excavated by John Storrie. (Source: Cardiff Naturalists Society.)

A second excavation of St Barruc's Chapel occurred during 1967–68, led by archaeologist Jeremy Knight, when the then Barry Borough Council decided that the area contiguous to the chapel should be developed as a park and the remains of the chapel, which were overgrown, should be tidied and re-excavated in a bid to not only gather information about the enshrinement of St Barruc, but to also further understand the chronology of the site. Although Storrie's excavation was thorough and methodical, much of the archaeological data recovered from his excavation was little understood at the time and was misinterpreted, leading to erroneous interpretations of the chapel's history and usage. This excavation gave archaeologists an opportunity to provide an updated interpretation and synthesis of the various stages of the chapel's construction and usage, but also its antecedents, giving us for the first time a very clear picture of the life of the chapel dedicated to St Barruc.

The first stone chapel dedicated to St Barruc appears to have been constructed sometime during the early twelfth century, and it is from this period that the earliest written reference to St Barruc's Chapel exists, coming to us from Giraldus Cambrensis in his *Journey Through Wales*, written 1188:

> Not far from Caerdyf is a small island situated near the shore of the Severn, called Barri, from St Baroc, who formerly lived there, and who's remains are deposited in a chapel overgrown with ivy, having been transferred to a coffin.

It seems that the Normans who established their manor nearby during the early twelfth century and Giraldus was seemingly related to, took their name from the island, as Giraldus states: 'From hence a noble family, of the maritime parts of South Wales, owned this island and the adjoining estates, received the name of de Barri'.

Giraldus also makes reference to a curious geographical feature in the near vicinity of St Barruc's Chapel, stating that:

> It is remarkable that, in a rock near the entrance of the island, there is a small cavity, to which, if the ear is applied, a noise is heard like that of smiths at work, the blowing of bellows, strokes of hammers, grinding of tools, and the roaring of furnaces; and it might easily be imagined that such noises, which are continued at the flow of the tides, were occasioned by the influx of the sea water under the cavities of the rocks.

Despite this description, there has never been such a cavity known on Barry Island, although a similar cavity does exit at Worm's Head in the Gower, suggesting that Giraldus received some of his information second hand and perhaps never actually visited Barry Island.

The Norman chapel simply consisted of a rectangular-shaped nave measuring 5.9 metres by 3.3 metres, and an apsidal-ended chancel that measured 3.4 metres and was roofed with locally sourced Pennant sandstone.

There exists evidence that a stone coffin was utilised during the Norman period to house the remains of St Barruc – perhaps the very coffin mentioned by Giraldus. This coffin was constructed with neatly dressed blocks of Jurassic limestone ashlar and was located in the southern end of the chancel.

It is possible that the Norman structure was constructed with funds provided by the recently arrived de Barri family, or Giraldus's 'noble family of the maritime parts of South Wales' whom Giraldus states 'owned Barry Island at this time'. It was indeed a common occurrence for noble patrons to grant religious establishments gifts, particularly land, during the medieval period. A notable local example of this type of patronage is the land at Ewenny Priory, which was given to the Benedictine religious order by William de Londres of Ogmore in the early twelfth century. The Norman chapel was in use until the early fourteenth century, when both the Norman nave and most of the chancel, a small part of which survives incorporated into the later period structure, were torn down and rebuilt.

DID YOU KNOW?

Although initially owned by the de Barry family, throughout the majority of the medieval and post-medieval periods, Barry Island was a part of the parish of Sully. It seems, however, that this occurrence did not impact on the day-to-day running of the chapel as there is no evidence to suggest that any sort of tithe was extracted from it or that it was interfered with in any way.

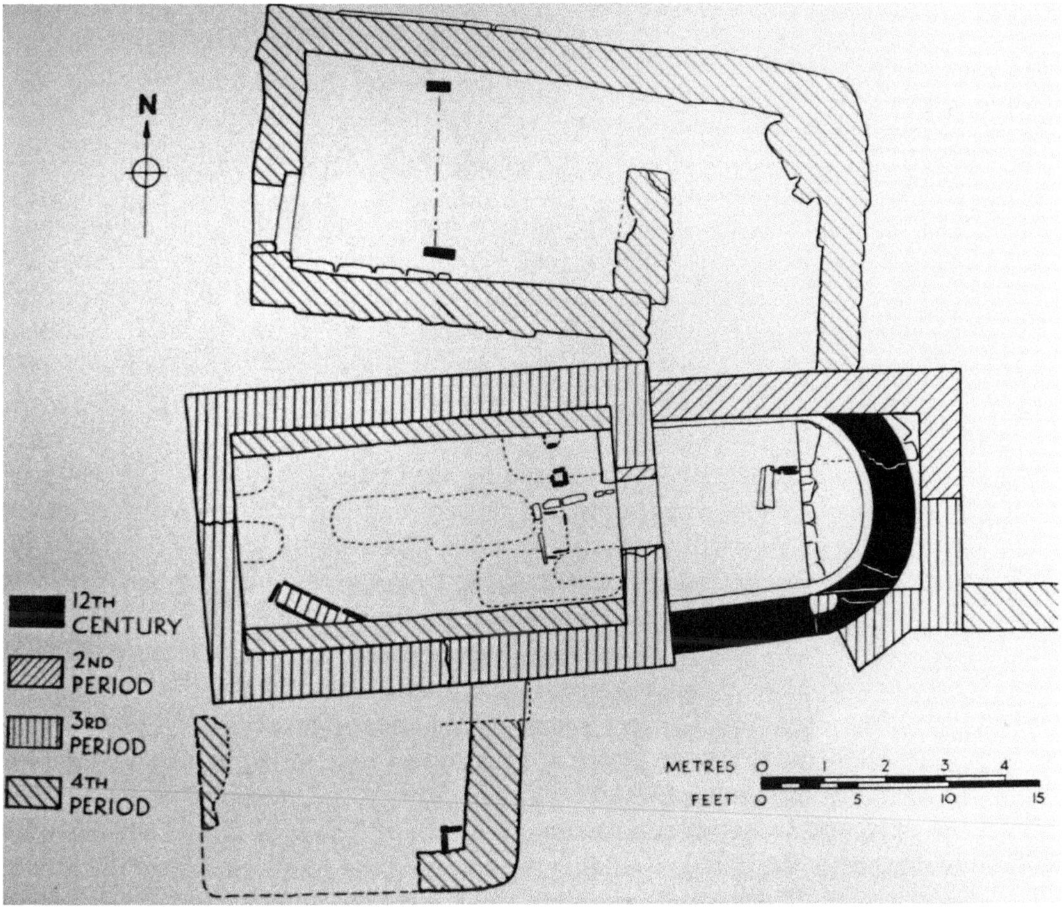

St Barruc's Chapel plan outlining the various stages of construction. (Source: Cardiff Naturalists Society.)

The early fourteenth century must have been a particularly prosperous time as the resident clergy evidently felt that the chapel could use a makeover in the latest architectural style – perhaps the old Norman structure was becoming dilapidated and unsafe or perhaps it was felt that the Decorated Gothic style was more fitting than the plain and bold Romanesque style that the Normans were so fond of. This was by no means an uncommon occurrence, as examples of this type of architectural modification exist at many religious establishments throughout Wales, with two good local examples existing at Llandaff Cathedral and St Illtyd's at Llantwit Major respectively, as well as on a larger scale at Tintern Abbey.

The new rebuild was similar in both shape and plan to the earlier Norman structure in that the new chapel, like its predecessor, consisted of simply a chancel and nave, with the new chancel being square-ended in shape and measuring 4.1 metres thick east–west by 3 metres north–south, and the nave, measuring 3.30 metres by 5.95 metres internally, complete with a handsome trefoil-headed lancet window. Both chancel and nave were fully excavated by Storrie, and at the time showed traces of wall paintings, a common

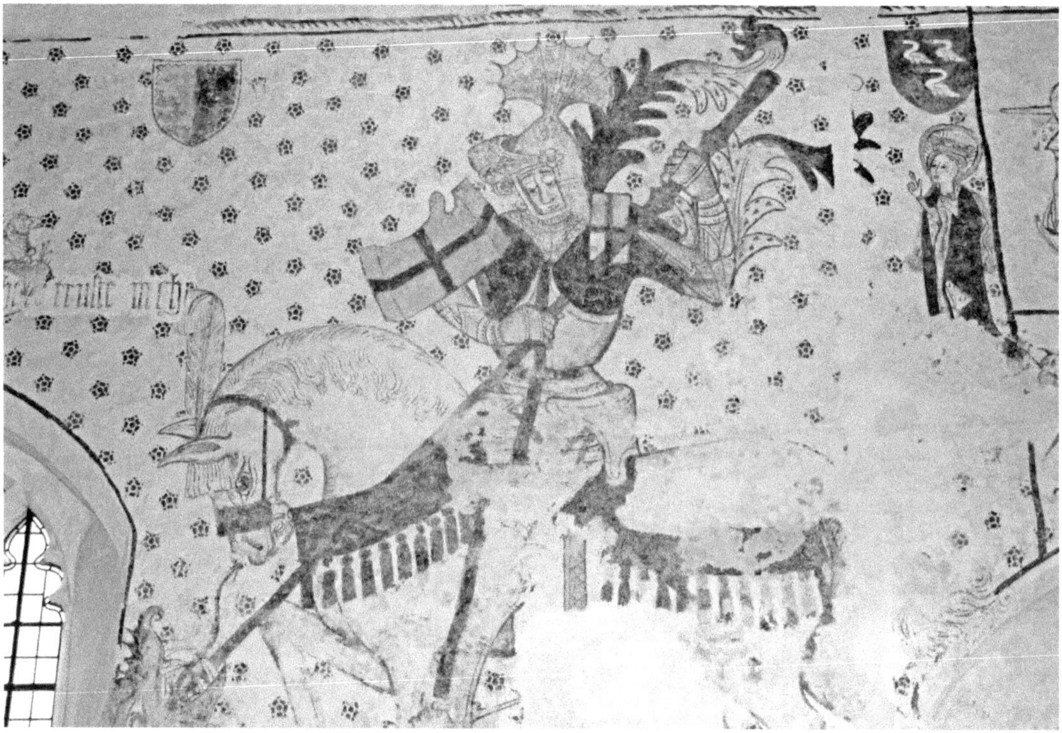

Late medieval wall painting of St George from Llancarfan Church.

feature in medieval churches throughout Wales. The interior of St Barruc's Chapel would have been a colourful place as its walls would have been painted with scenes from the Bible and religious themes such as the paintings recently discovered and preserved on the walls of St Cadoc's Church, Llancarfan.

It would appear that when the chapel was rebuilt it was given a new roof of blue Cornish slate, topped with green-glazed ridge tiles, replacing the Pennant sandstone used to roof the Norman period building. As part of the fourteenth-century makeover, a porch measuring 2.50 metres by 3.45 metres internally was added on the south side of the nave. Excavations have shown that the porch was a timber-framed structure and that it was torn down before both the chapel and cemetery went out of use, as a later burial was found cut through its north-east angle.

Not long after the chapel was rebuilt, however, the whole southern half of the chancel's east wall was torn down and rebuilt. In addition, parts of both the east and south chancel walls were rebuilt from the foundations up. Several buttresses were constructed to support the rebuilt walls – the issue of stability was clearly an important one. Knight's excavations showed the rebuilding to be necessitated by structural instabilities, most likely caused by both loose sandy soil and burial cuts that together served to help undermine the new foundations.

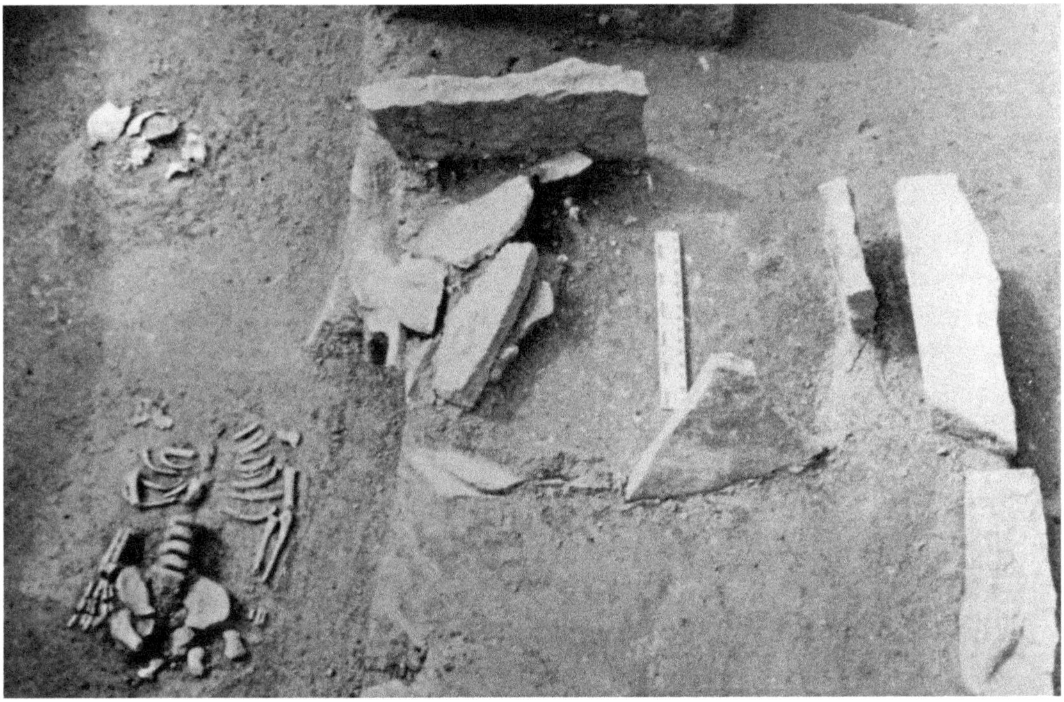

Alter complex with associated skeletal remains discovered during Knight's excavation. (Source: Cardiff Naturalists Society.)

Internally the rebuilt chapel contained an alter complex, complete with stone relic cavity, located within the east end of the nave in front of the chancel arch. This structure had, however, gone out of use before the church was abandoned as two graves were found cut into it on the south side. The chapel also contained a series of stone benches constructed on the north and south walls, and a font drain. The stone coffin that was in existence during the Norman period was probably destroyed during one of the fourteenth century rebuilds, as fragments of this coffin were found inserted into the chancel floor among rubble used to help support the structural rebuild. A fragment of a stone relic container was also found inserted into the fourteenth-century stone paving in the chancel area.

The fourteenth century also saw the construction of a priest's house, which lay contiguous to the chapel on the north side. Knight believed that Storrie had misinterpreted this building as being an 'oratory' dating to the fifth century, a misunderstanding stemming from the fact that Storrie believed the construction of the building to be unsophisticated, and also due to the fact that Storrie found fragments of Roman tile and bricks incorporated into the structure and a Roman coin in the near vicinity. The priest's house consisted of low sleeper walls and, like the chapel, was a modest structure that was divided into two sections, with the main 'hall' measuring 5.20 metres by 3.15 metres internally and a separate room – probably a sleeping chamber – measuring 2.4 metres long.

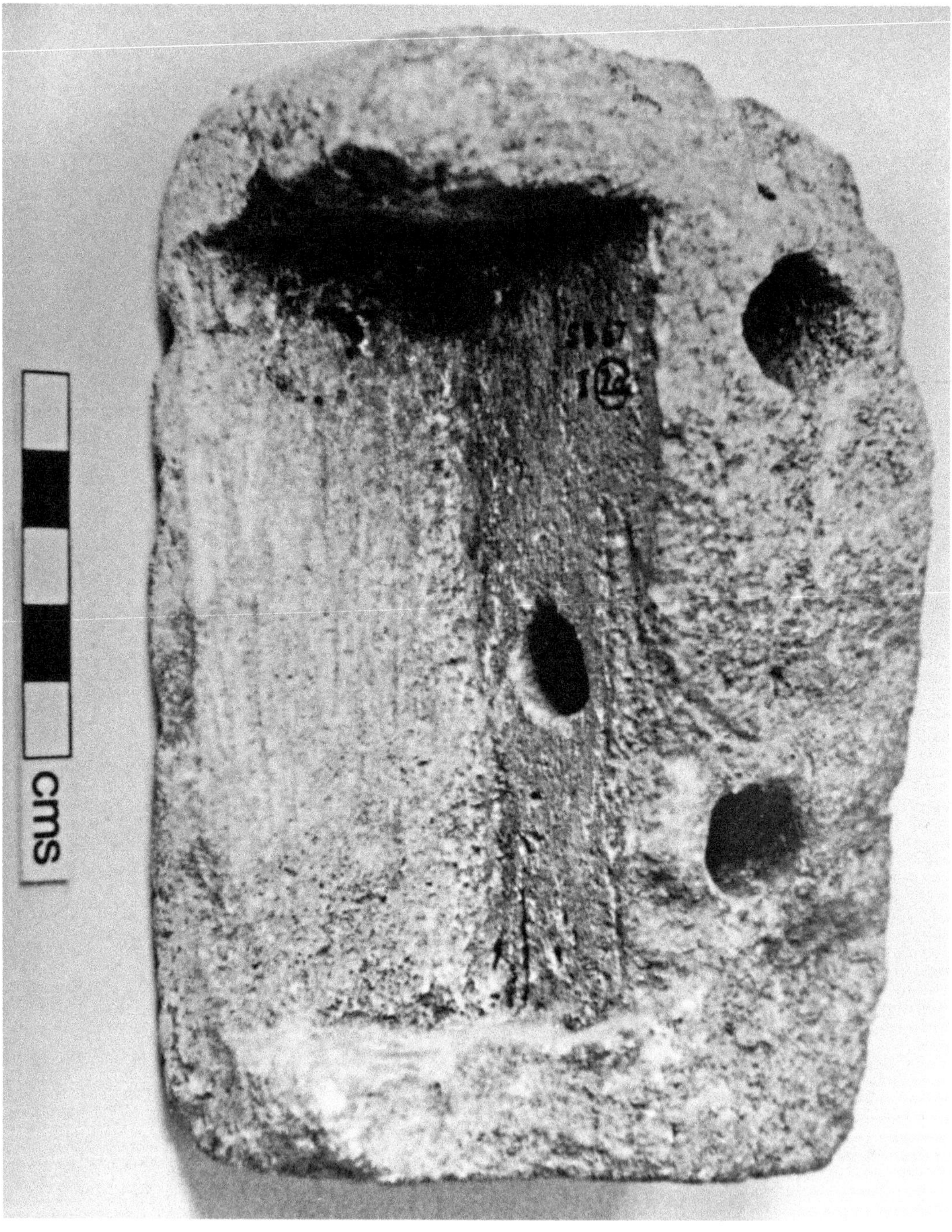

Half of a stone relic container found during Knight's excavation. (Source: Cardiff Naturalists Society.)

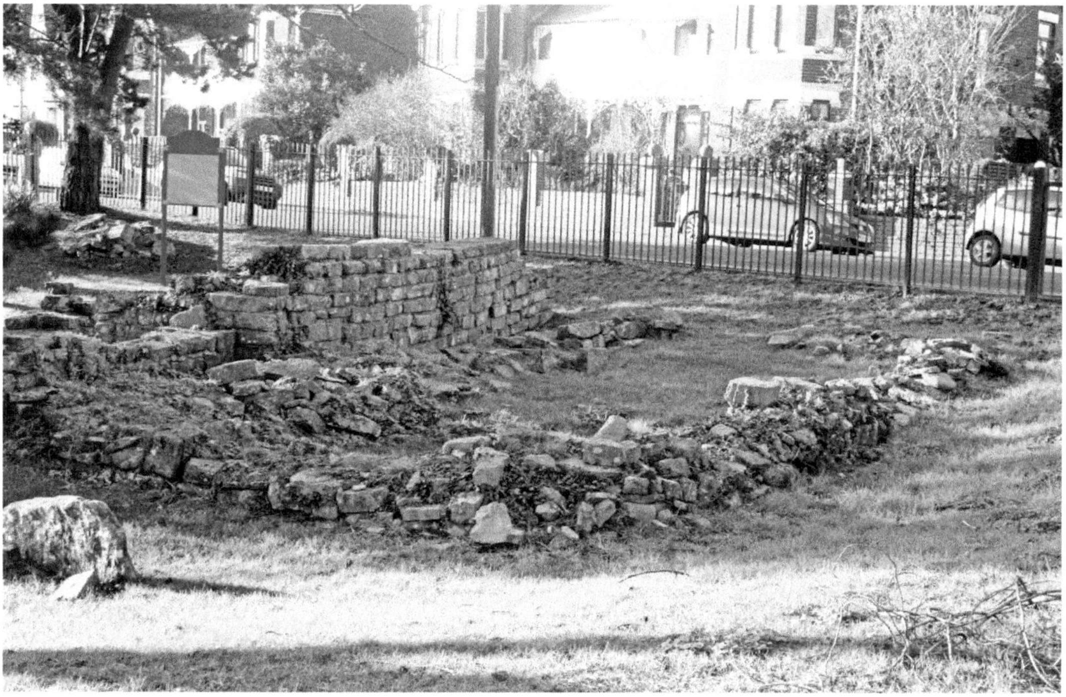

View of the fourteenth-century priest's house.

DID YOU KNOW?

St Barruc's Chapel was unusual in that it was not affiliated within the episcopate of Llandaff or indeed with any other religious governance, such as the various religious orders that had houses throughout Wales during the medieval period. It was, in essence, a free church, and as such existed purely on the donations of both patrons and pilgrims. Evidence for this unusual occurrence can be found by noting the absence of St Barruc's Chapel from the Norwich Taxation of 1254, the Taxatio of 1291 and the Valor Ecclesiasticus of 1535 – none of which make reference to St Barruc's Chapel.

The chapel by this time was probably how it appeared to Leland during the early sixteenth century when he spoke of the 'fair little chapel of St Barrok', as it was during this period when the popularity of St Barruc's Chapel reached its zenith. The architectural embellishments and modifications undertaken during the fourteenth century serve as a reflection of how popular the chapel was with pilgrims, who presumably donated generously.

The area surrounding the chapel was in use as a cemetery for at least as long as the stone-built chapel was in existence. The exact area that comprised the cemetery, however, is unknown, as most of the immediate environs surrounding the chapel have been built over. It is, however, thought to have been extensive and to have stretched towards the east and north. Several of the burials from the cemetery were encountered and excavated by John Storrie when sewer trenches were being dug on Friars Road during the late nineteenth century. Residents living in the houses on Friars Road opposite St Barruc's Chapel have also reported finding skeletal remains while gardening.

During both excavations great care was taken to not disturb the majority of the burials; only burials encountered during excavations of the chapel and immediate surroundings were excavated. The burials that were excavated, however, were all standard east–west Christian burials, unaccompanied by objects. Some of the burials predated the Norman chapel, such as those that were excavated by Storrie under the Norman masonry.

It would appear that St Barruc's Chapel was not the only building on Barry Island during the medieval period, as John Storrie had the opportunity to examine other remains located roughly where the modern fairground is today. These remains consisted of a series of low-lying walls that were constructed of lias rubble, with an associated paved area

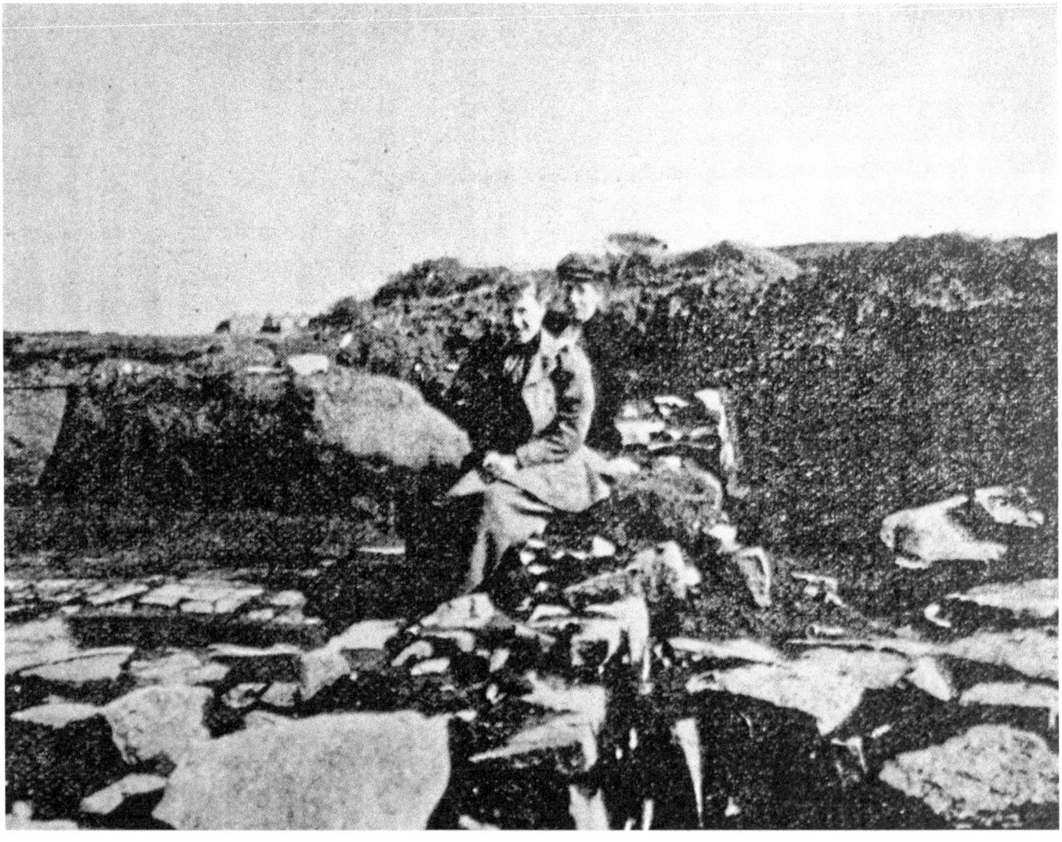

Late nineteenth-century view of the 'The Early Abbey'. (Source: Cardiff Naturalists Society.)

located nearby. Also discovered was a hearth and various fragments of medieval pottery dating to the thirteenth and fourteenth centuries. Parts of this complex were divided into seven enclosures measuring roughly 2.4 metres with a width of approximately 0.9 metres.

It is possible that these remains could have served as lodgings for some of the pilgrims who visited the island, or were perhaps used as farm buildings and housed agricultural workers, animals, or perhaps both – a medieval ridge and furrow field system exists at nearby Friars Point to support this theory.

Most of the people who used the chapel were probably from the Glamorgan area; for example, a letter written in March 1476 by local man Sir Harry Stradling of St Donats while in Rome, implores his wife 'to se my dayes kept at Barry, for ye days must nede be kept, or else I must be schaymed'. It is also possible that people from further afield, including visiting sailors arriving at the nearby port of Barry, might have also paid a visit to St Barruc's Chapel. Interestingly, a lead episcopal bulla of Giraud de Libra, Bishop of Vaison (1271–95), was found on the island by a local resident in 1948. This episcopal bulla would have been used to grant an indulgence or privilege to its recipient – perhaps a mariner whose vessel was anchored at Barry Harbour opposite Ostry Bay, or a Glamorgan pilgrim. The bulla was eventually acquired by the museum in 1955.

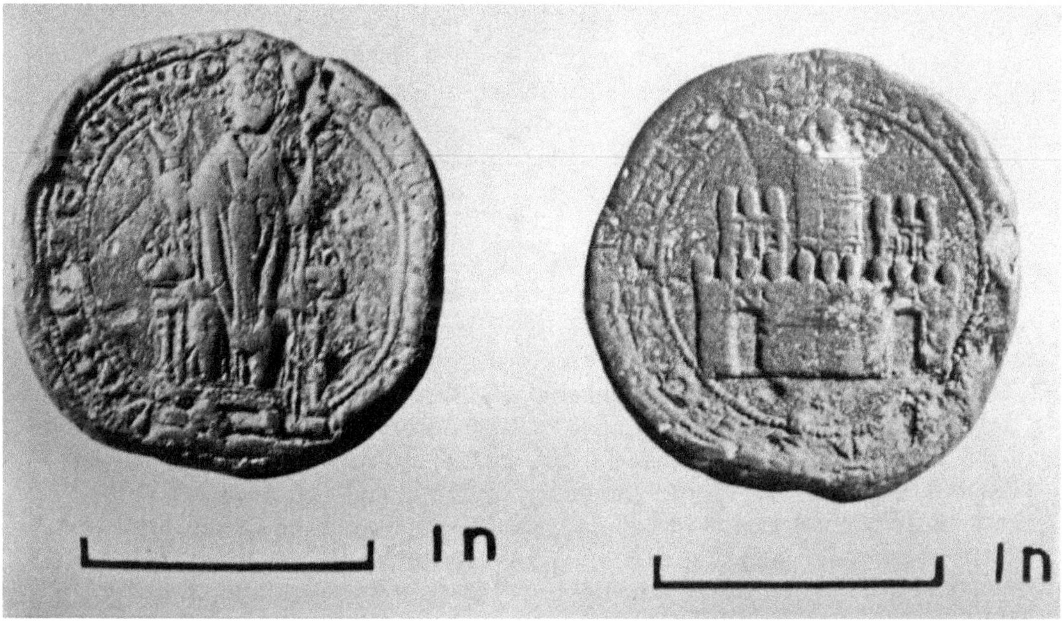

Medieval episcopal bulla found on Barry Island in 1948. (Source: Cardiff Naturalists Society.)

7. Post-Medieval Period

Ruins and Solitude

When Leland visited Barry Island during the early sixteenth century, the scene greeting him from the mainland would not have changed much from this early photo from 1884. St Barruc's Chapel, though, would have declined as a place of pilgrimage, as an account of Leland's visit in his book *The Itinerary in Wales of John Leland* (1536–39) intimates, 'There ys no dwelling in the isle, but ther is in the midle of it a fair litle chapel of S. Barrok, wher much pilgrimage was used.' This decline was precipitated by a lack of pilgrims and those wishing to use the services the chapel offered. The schism from the Catholic Church in Rome in 1532 and the rise of Protestantism and the Church of England caused great civil unrest in Britain. These events no doubt helped to contribute towards the decline of St Barruc's Chapel, as by this time saints, miracles, and shrines had declined in popularity; anything associated with Catholicism was suppressed, notably during the Reformation, and particularly during the reign of Edward VI. Lack of pilgrims meant a lack of money, without which the chapel could simply not have survived, and indeed it didn't – its decline was slow but certain.

In addition to noting St Barruc's Chapel, Leland took care to also take note of the setting and topography of Barry Island. He wrote:

> Right againe this brooke mouth lyith Barrey Isle. The passage into it at ful se is a flite shot over, as much as the Tamise is over the bridge. At low water ther is a broken causey to go over, or else' over the shalow stremelet of Barrey brooke on the sandes". "The Isle is about a mile in cumpace, and hath very good corne, grasse and sum wood. The ferme of it worthe a x. li. a yeare.

Despite Leland's visit, it would seem that not a great deal happened on Barry Island during the sixteenth and seventeenth centuries; farming it seems was the major preoccupation of all who had any vested interest in Barry Island at this time.

According to the early Glamorganshire antiquarian Rice Meyrick, by the mid-sixteenth century Barry Island was the home of numerous rabbit warrens. In the

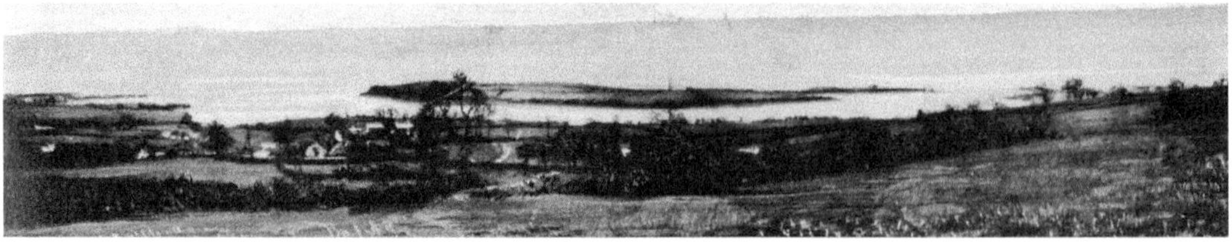

An 1884 photograph depicting Barry Island from the mainland. (Source: Tom Clements.)

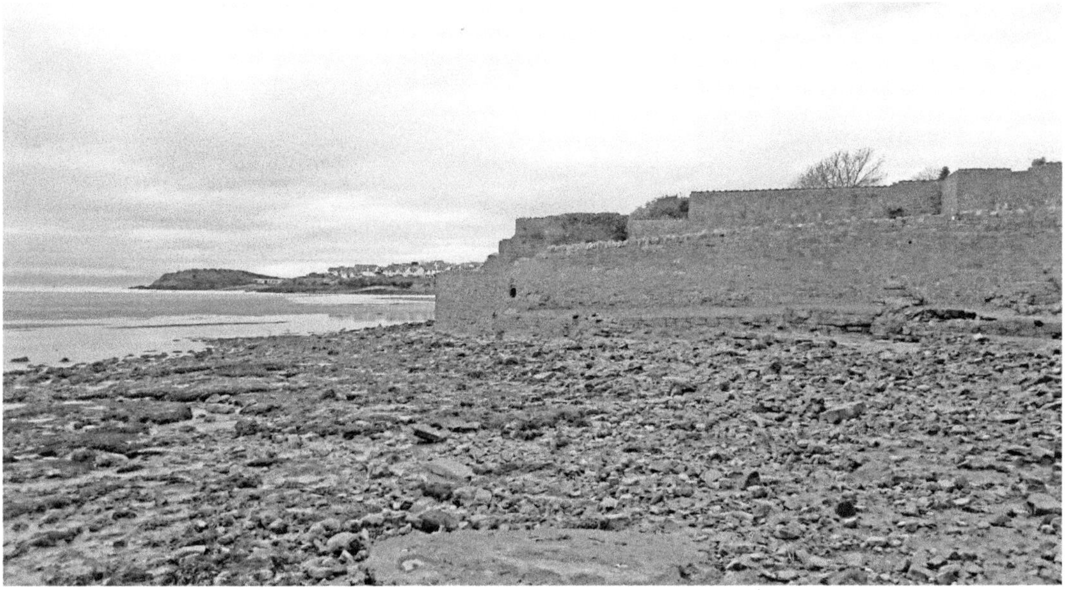

The remains of the old port of Barry.

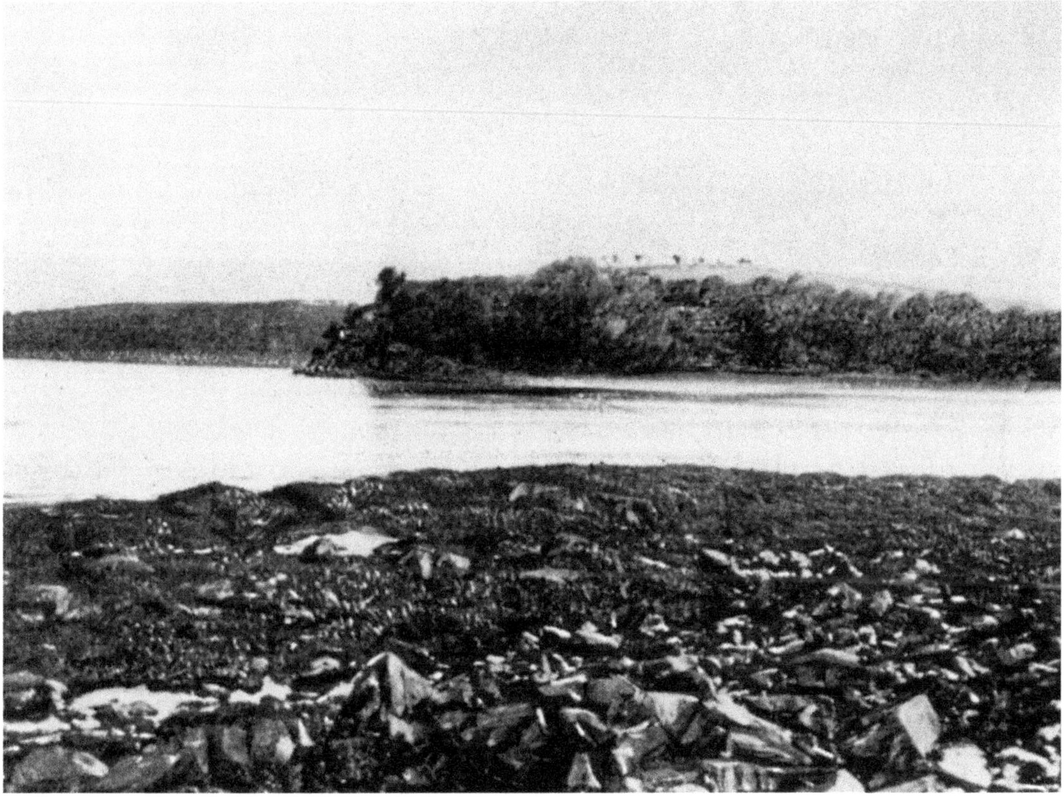

View of Barry Sound and Castleland from Barry Island. (Source: Tom Clements.)

year 1551 Barry Island appears in a grant conferred upon William Herbert of Cogan Pill by Edward VI. Interestingly, this grant mentions a 'fee of Ralph Jonson', keeper of the island, or 'warren of Barrey'. Barry Island it seems had been under royal control for some time prior to William Herbert's acquisition, as during the late fifteenth century Barry Island was held by one Duke Jasper of Bedford and was included in a package of lands forming the lordship of Glamorgan. It was upon Jasper's death in 1495 that the Crown acquired Barry Island. Barry Island was to remain with the Herbert family well into the seventeenth century.

DID YOU KNOW?

After a heavy storm during August 1987 an interesting discovery of twelve 'merida-type' pottery vessels was made in the tidal mud of Jackson's Bay. These pottery vessels, which date to the sixteenth or seventeenth centuries, are thought to have come from the Iberian Peninsula and originally held wine or oil. How these vessels came to end up in Jackson's Bay, however, is a mystery.

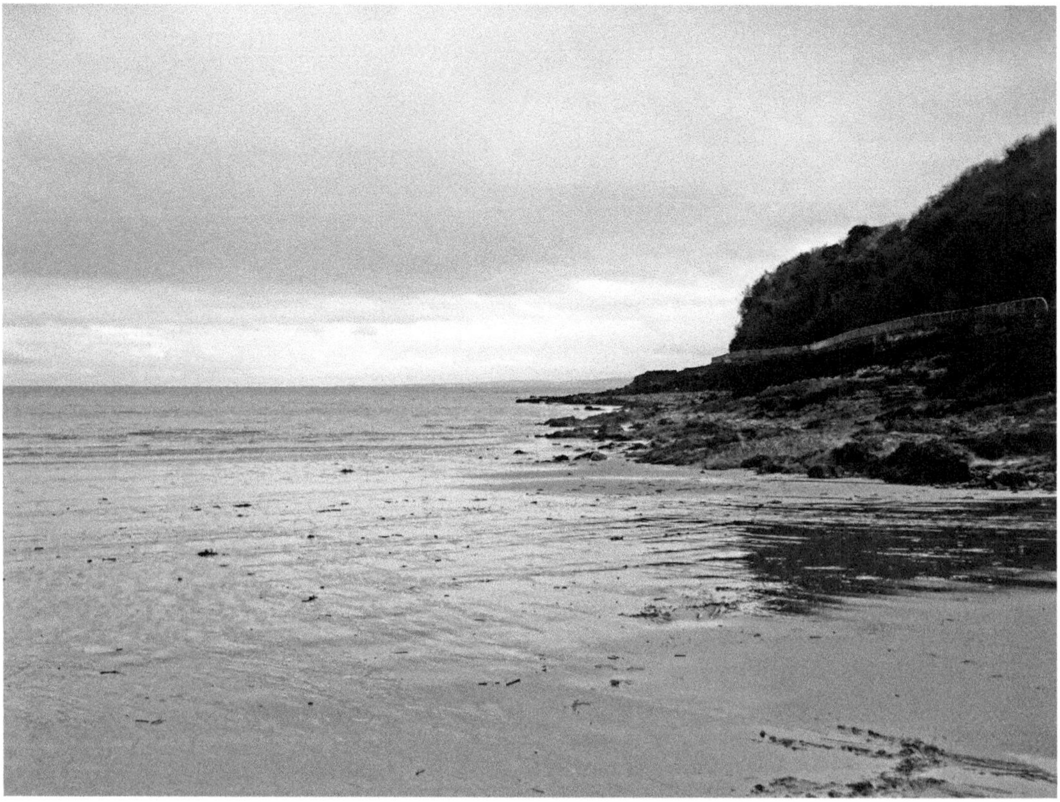

Jackson's Bay.

The year 1666 saw Barry Island's owner, one Philip Jones of Fonmon, assign its lease to local gentleman David Spencer of Merthyr Dyfan. It is David Spencer's son, also called David Spencer, who wrote his late seventeenth-century account of his visit to Barry Island for posterity.

By the late seventeenth century the chapel of St Barruc was a ruin, as David Spencer asserted: 'There is ye ruins of a chapel'. The sequence of medieval buildings located where the fairground is today were also ruinous, having been long neglected and abandoned, as David Spencer records that there were 'ye ruins of many houses'. Curiously, these ruins were also noted by Samuel Lewis in his mid-nineteenth-century publication *A Topographical Dictionary of Wales*, where they were interpreted as being 'two ancient chapels'. In addition to taking note of archaeological features, David Spencer also took time to record the topography of the island; it would seem that it had changed little since Leland's visit. He states:

> [The island was] now inhabited only with one house. It breeds very good cattle and sheep and there are plenty of rabbits on it. It is also good for corn, wheat, barley and pease. Also good for fishing belonging to it of plays and soules and millet and base. Also good fowling on it.

The ruins of St Barruc's Chapel remained visible well into the eighteenth century, as an estate map from 1762 attests to, which was commissioned by Barry Island's then owner Sir Edmund Thomas of Wenvoe. Another map dating to 1798, once again commissioned by the Wenvoe estate's then owner, Mr Peter Birt, who purchased the estate in 1774, also

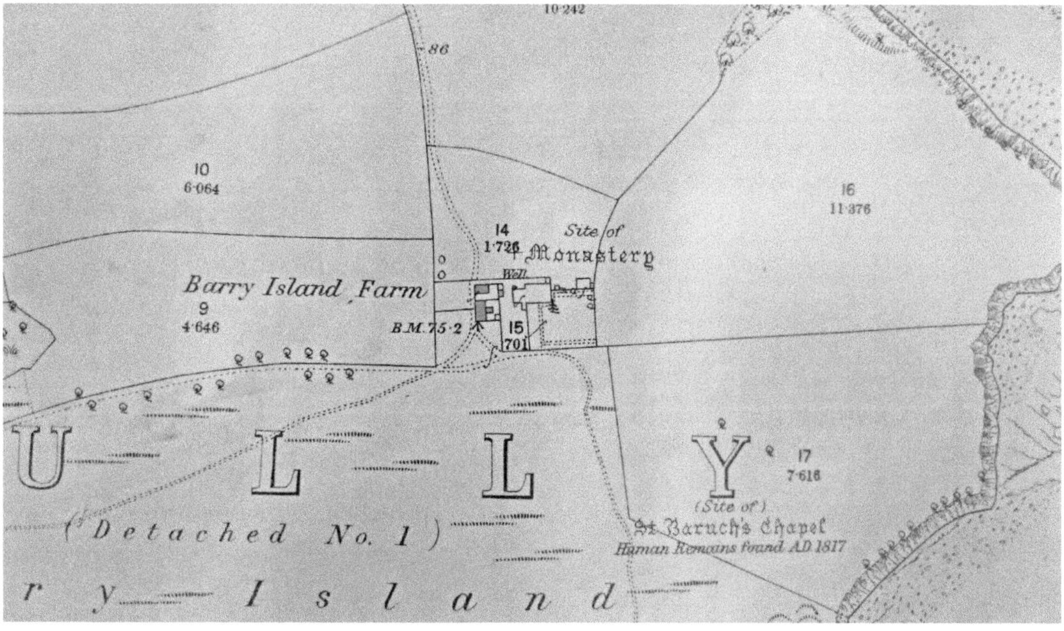

The location where the old farmhouse stood. (Source: Glamorgan Archives.)

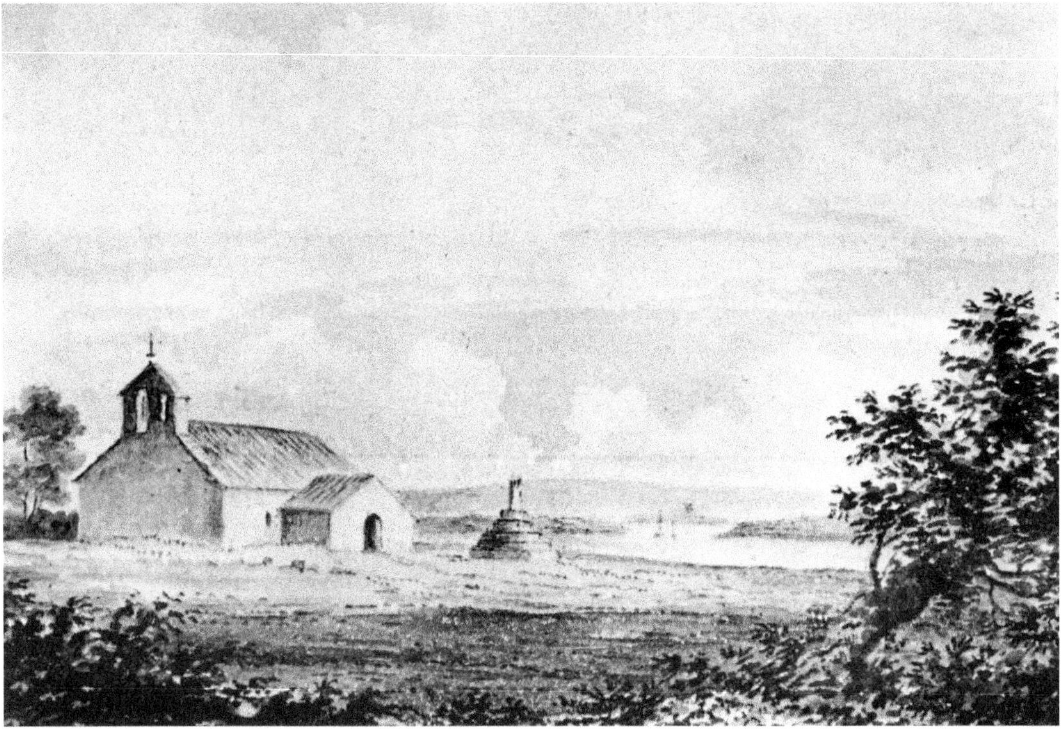

Early nineteenth-century view of Barry Island. (Source: Tom Clements.)

depicts the ruins of St Barruc's Chapel; however, by the time Revd J. Evans visited in 1804 the chapel had disappeared completely.

The map drawn up in 1762 is particularly interesting as it takes note of all features of interest; for example, it shows us that there were four enclosed fields on Ostry Hill at this time, the rest of the island, however, probably consisted of rough pasture. The map also shows us that there was a small pool located near to Ostry Bay marked on the 1762 map as 'Leach Pool'. In addition to showing the ruins of St Barruc's Chapel, the map also shows us the location of St Barruc's Well, which was noted by David Spencer, as we have previously seen, as 'a well of very good water', although curiously not the 'Roman well' excavated by Storrie or the medieval ruins thought by Storrie to be 'The Early Abbey'.

The only building in use on Barry Island during the post-medieval period was a small farmhouse that was located near the summit of Ostry Hill on the east side of the island, and is curiously noted on several nineteenth-century OS maps as 'Site of Monastery'. This building was in existence from the mid- to late seventeenth century until the late nineteenth century, with the stone used in its construction probably taken from the defunct St Barruc's Chapel and thus contributing towards the appearance the chapel exhibits today. The occupants of the farmhouse were tenant farmers who took their lease from the various owners of the island, the majority of whom, as we have seen, were comprised of the local gentry.

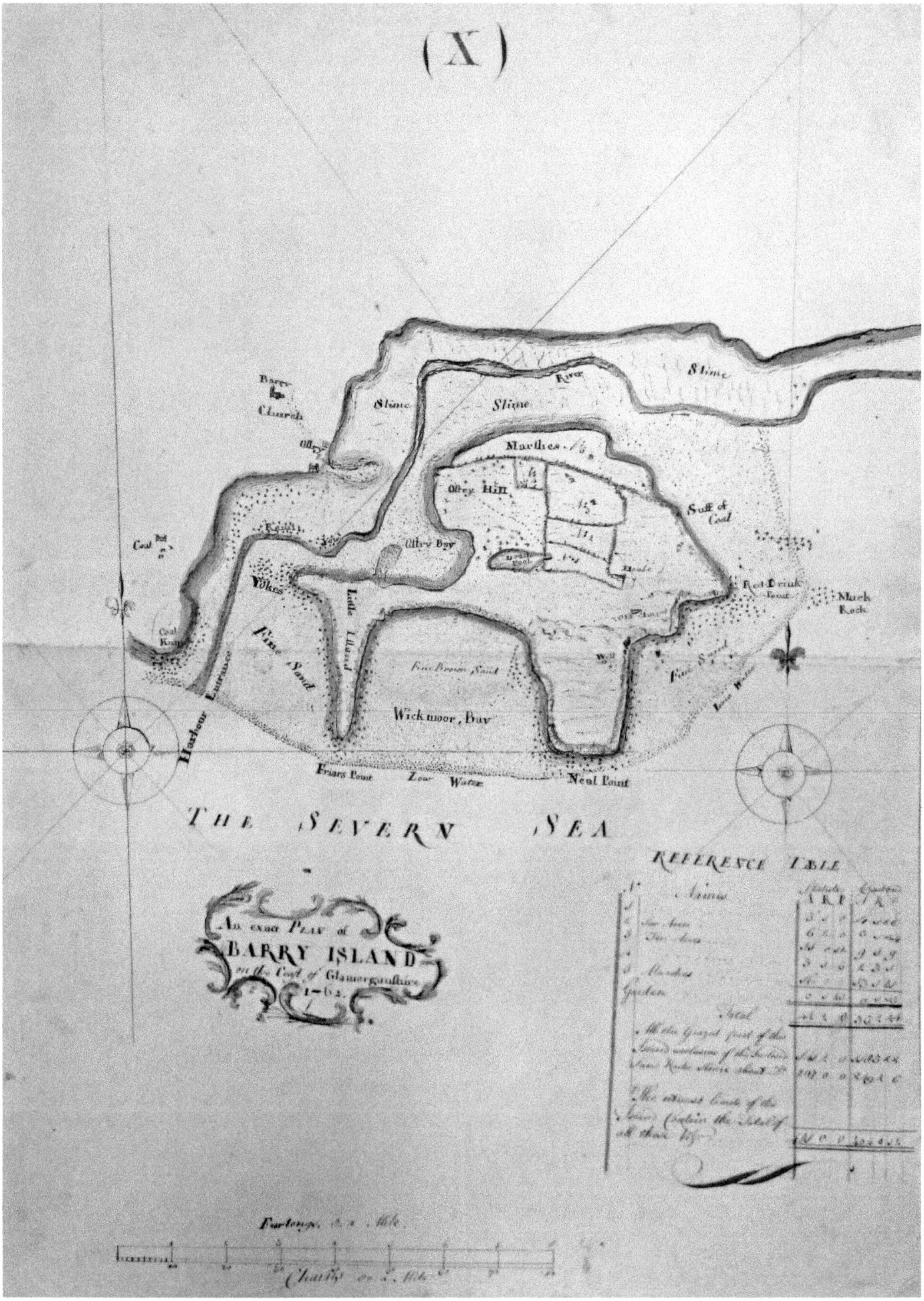

Eighteenth-century estate map of Barry Island. (Source: Glamorgan Archives.)

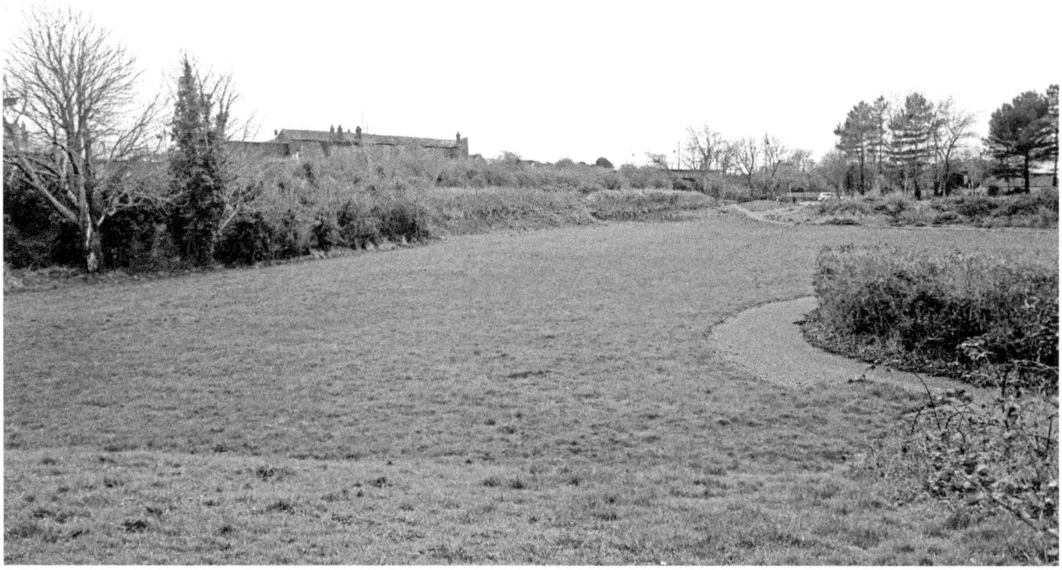

Location of where the leach pool once existed.

8. Smugglers

It is perhaps the ambiance and isolation that Barry Island provided that gave impetus to the most infamous chapter in Barry Island's otherwise peaceful history – that of its association with smuggling.

Smuggling was endemic along the entire coastline of Britain, and the south Wales coast was no exception. For a time Barry Island became a notorious place where customs officials feared to tread.

The presence of customs officials throughout the locality seems to have provided little or no deterrent to prevent smuggling, much of which was attempted surreptitiously, but some of which was also very brazen. This is not all that surprising considering that the smugglers were probably aided by, or at the least had the sympathy of, much of the local population, many of whom would also have stood to gain through association with smuggling and looting. The smugglers attempted to conceal a variety of contraband such as tea, rum, brandy, port, tobacco, as well as more unusual items such as wool, soap, counterfeit coins, china, and human hair.

DID YOU KNOW?

The late seventeenth century saw a drastic hike in customs duties and the introduction of a new tax called 'excise' (a tax on domestic consumption), which caused the cost of both luxury items and everyday products to suddenly become very expensive. As the eighteenth century progressed, successive governments saw fit to steadily increase these unwanted taxes – something that was greatly resented by the vast majority of Britain's population, most of whom were poor. This occurrence was directly responsible for the huge rise in smuggling that was prevalent throughout Britain during the eighteenth century.

A good example of the population's duplicity occurred in the year of 1737 when two vessels returning with tobacco from Virginia floundered at Nash Point and were subject to their cargo being looted; customs officials wrote:

> The mob was very insolent, not only pilfering the damaged hogsheads in spite of the officers, but even burning the hull to get at the old iron, three or four hundred people assembled there every night from all parts of the country towards the hills: particularly

> from a place called Bridgend, from whence came a gang of ruffians the last day the proclamation was read.

Apprehending the looters was no easy task, with officials at Cardiff stating that the deputy sheriff required an 'extraordinary gratuity' in order to pursue the Bridgend looters and that 'they will never be taken, for he [deputy sheriff] must run the risque of his life, there being no less than thirty or forty of the mob that live together in a little town called Bridgend in this county'. Indeed, the deputy sheriff himself was suspected of being friends with the Bridgend looters and therefore complicit in the looting.

Such was the risk in apprehending these men that professional soldiers from Swansea demanded no less than £20 per man in order to detain two of the worst individuals associated with the Bridgend mob, namely one Edward David and Lazarus George, both described as being 'very desperate people'. In view of the risk associated with apprehending smugglers, the collector at the port of Cardiff, in the year 1743, suggested that the seven preventative officer's stationed there should be provided with an array of weapons, namely 'a pair of pistols, a hanger [sword] and a short gun of three foot'.

These events give us some idea what Cardiff customs officials were up against on a regular basis and the scale of smuggling and looting that occurred on the south Wales coast. In short, the customs officials were outnumbered and sometimes, quite literally, outgunned for much of the duration of their existence, making their job an extremely dangerous one.

In the year 1732 Cardiff customs officials wrote to the board in London that 'smugglers do begin in this channel to appear already, and about a fortnight ago there was one of them, of Aberthaw and Barry, but no boat did venture out to her'. The year 1734 saw smuggling activities grow bolder, as narrated by Cardiff customs officials in a letter once again to London:

> At Barry; if they find the officer on the iseland they'll land the other side of the harbour. If the other side of the harbour, they'll land on the iseland, and the officers cant get over till the tide is out, wchch may be five or six hours; and there is so much cover on the iseland, and such conveniencys for hiding of goods the other side, that an officer has but a poor chance to meet with em after they are landed.

A letter from Whitehall, London, dated 5 June 1735 gives Cardiff customs officials due notice of an illegal cargo of goods to arrive in the area, stating: 'A vessel is dayly expected at the Flat Holmes who is to come to an anchor there at night and send her goods ashore by her boat in order to be conceald till opportunity offers to carry them to other places.' It seems that Barry Island was a possible location as the Cardiff officers were directed to 'communicate this information to officers at the port of Barry and Sully and direct them to use their utmost endeavours to prevent these frauds reporting to us the success'.

The officers stationed at Cardiff it seems were alarmed by this surge in smuggling and as a result 'crave the appointment of an effective revenue cruiser'. The authorities in

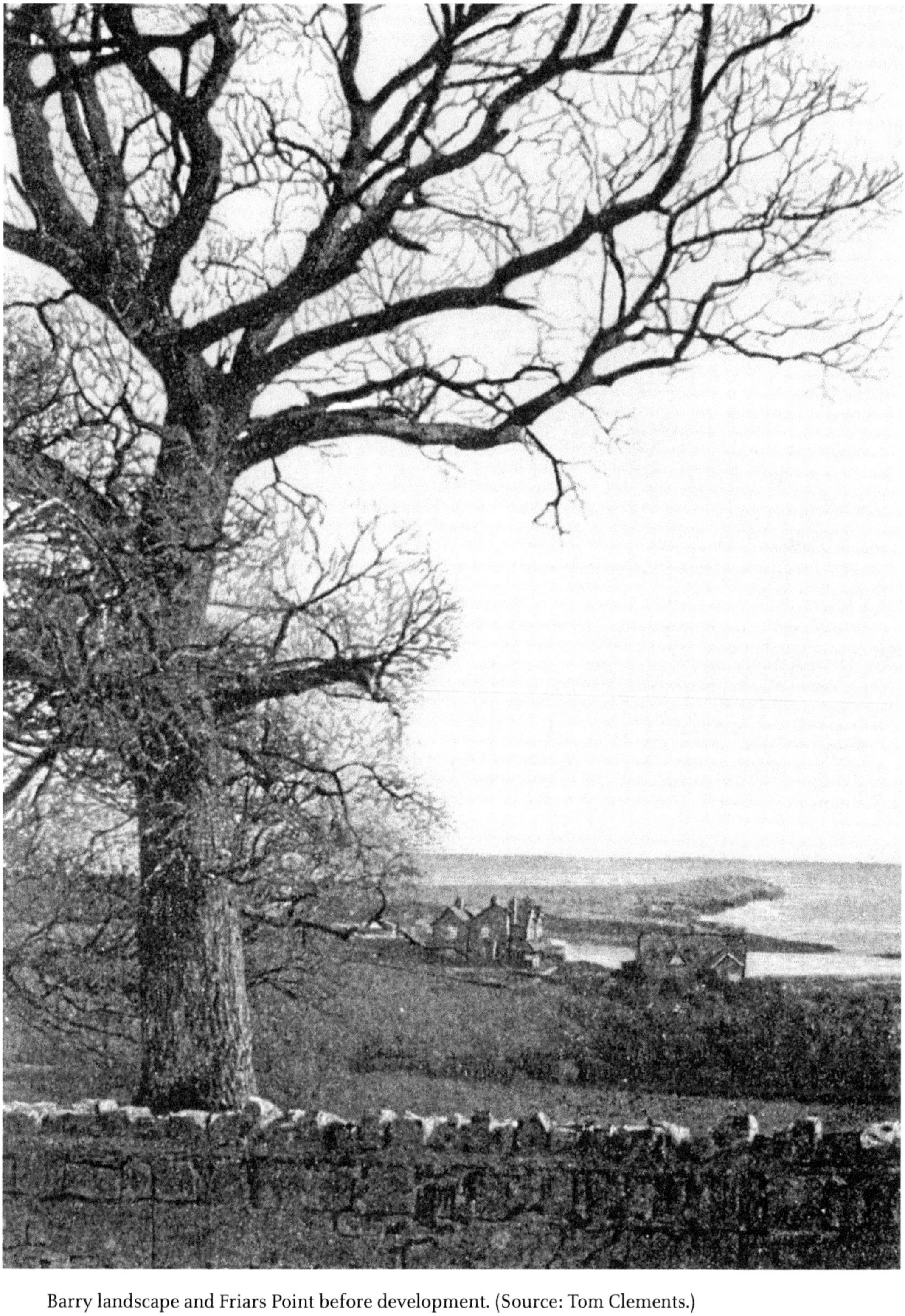

Barry landscape and Friars Point before development. (Source: Tom Clements.)

London, however, were satisfied that a single sloop stationed at Portishead, near Bristol, would be an adequate deterrent to prevent smuggling activity along the Bristol Channel and the south Wales coast.

DID YOU KNOW?

In the year 1760, the authorities discovered multiple barrels of brandy floating off Barry Island and washed up on Barry Island beach. Where these barrels came from was a mystery as there are no records to indicate any particular vessel had floundered in the vicinity, making it entirely possible (and highly probable) that these barrels were lost or discarded during an abortive smuggling undertaking. Local landowner Lady Windsor attempted to lay claim to the brandy as 'wreck', a part of her prerogative within the lordship of Cosmeston. The Admiralty, however, also attempted to claim the brandy as flotsam.

The year 1770 saw a government cutter involved in an attack, as is narrated in another letter to London:

> To William Richards Surveyor for going to acquaint the officers of the Waterguard at Penarth, Barry and Aberthaw of the Pelham Cutter being feloniously and piratically

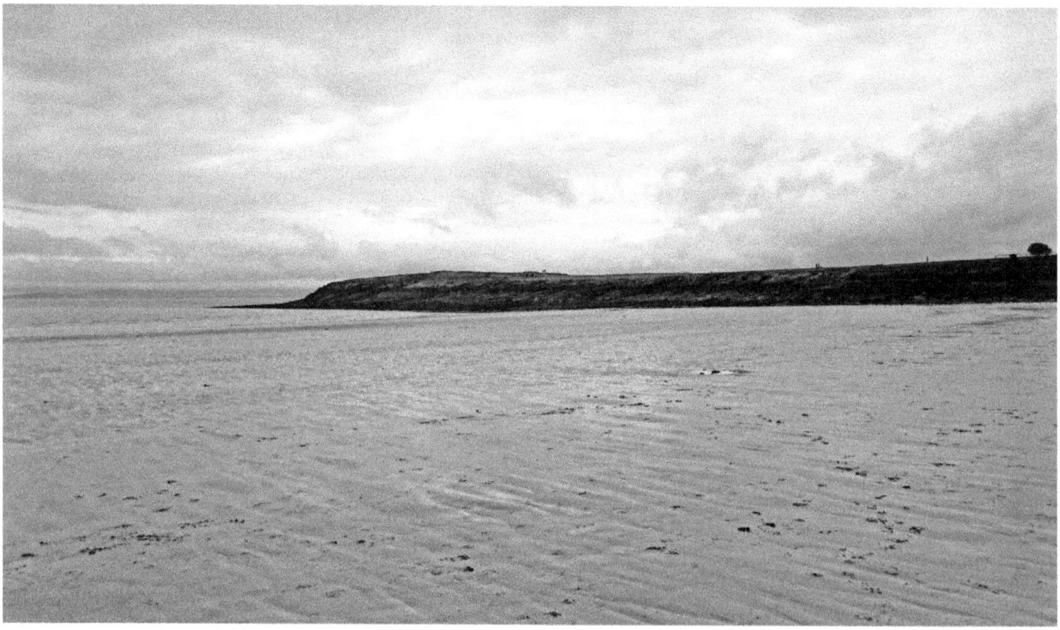

Whitmore Bay's isolation was conducive to smuggling contraband.

> attack'd and c; by two large smuggling cutters and a large wherry, with orders for them to keep a strict look out in order to apprehend the smugglers.

In the year 1784 Barry Island received the unwelcome attention of notorious smuggler Thomas Knight, who had decided to audaciously set up his base on the island – right under the noses of the revenue men. Knight was infamous throughout the south Wales area and brazenly conducted his smuggling activities all along the Welsh coast.

In 1784 customs officials attempted seized a cargo of wine on Barry Island, but were unsuccessful; a letter dated 3 April 1784 states that:

> Thomas Knight, a noted smuggler who resides a great part of his time on the said island, told Thomas Hopkins, waiter and searcher at Barry and Sully, that the wine should remain there; which wine on entering the house a second time was all removed from thence.

The building referred to in the letter must have been the farmhouse located on Ostry Hill, as this was the only building on Barry Island at this time. Quite what the occupants of the farm on Barry Island thought of Knight appropriating their home for his smuggling enterprise is unclear, although it's likely that they never had much of a choice in the matter. This incident was the first of many involving Knight and customs officials.

Complaints about Knight increased. A letter also written in 1784 tells us:

> The said Knight carries on a very considerable trade in the smuggling way, and is so strongly supported, that there are but particular times that I can venture to send my

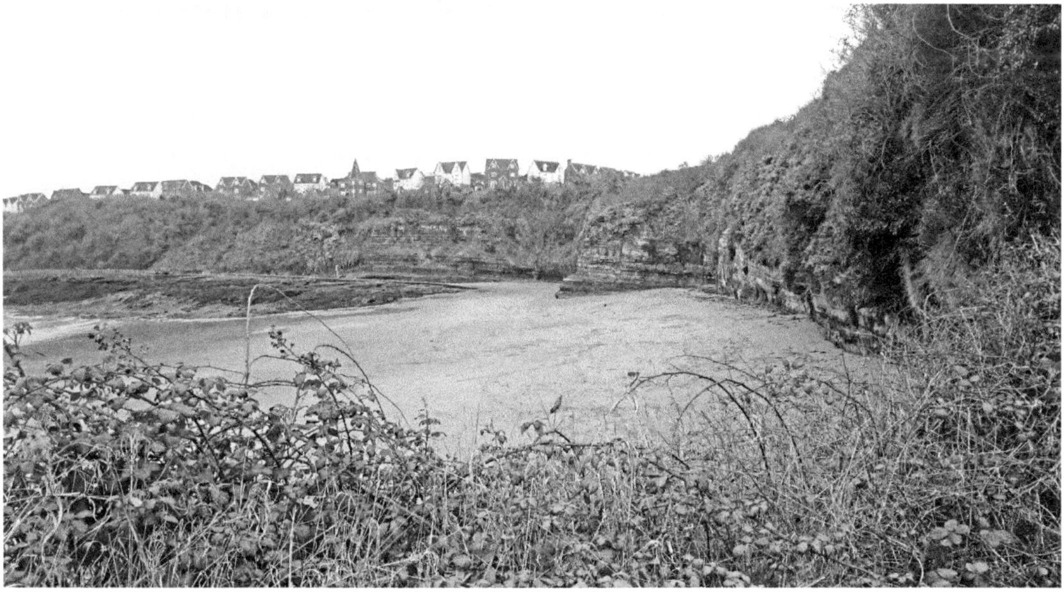

Jackson's Bay.

> officers to the said island, he has sometimes I am informed 60 or 70 men with him from on board a large cutter on the smuggling trade, which we suppose Knight to be the propriitor of.

On 17 April of the same year customs officials appear to have had even greater cause for concern as another letter states: 'Great activity amongst the smugglers ... A large cutter is now off the island of Barry of 24 guns and 35 men running goods on the said island.' In addition to this show of bravado, it appears Knight also held the local population of Barry in terror, which at the time consisted of a small village and associated port: 'Its with great truth we assure you that the people here are in such dread of Knight and his gang, that we found a difficulty in finding people to work for us,' stating that 'we can't conceive anybody has any business here, who is not connected with Knight and smuggling.'

Customs officials, however, were determined to do their best to apprehend Knight. A letter dated 18 November 1784 states that a large quantity of tobacco was seized, and in the following months customs officials confiscated the boat of a local man named 'Griffins', who was implicated with Knight's smuggling trade. Griffins, however, subsequently petitioned the customs officials for the return of his boat. It would appear that the tenacity of the customs officers eventually paid off and Knight was finally dislodged from Barry Island in 1785, as customs officials stated: 'Knight, the smuggler, is now at Lundy Island, having been driven from Barry, the protection of his armed brig being removed, smuggling has greatly diminished here.'

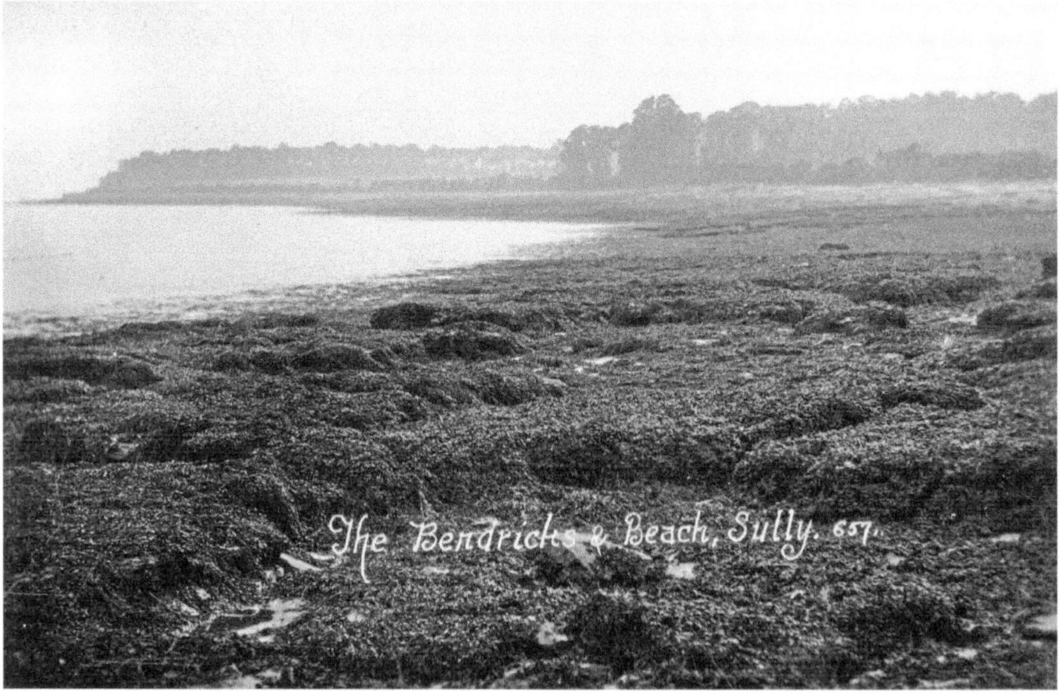

Barry Island as seen from The Bendricks. (Source: Tom Clements.)

It is unclear what became of Knight but the authorities managed to apprehend and detain one of Knight's associates, a local man named Thomas Bennett 'formerly of Barry Island', and fined him the hefty sum of £173 for being in possession of smuggled goods. Whether or not Thomas was coerced into helping Knight or was a willing participant is unclear, but this sum proved too much for Thomas to pay, and by the year 1786 it seems Thomas was languishing in a debtor's prison at Cardiff.

It would appear that Knight's departure afforded customs officials a brief respite from the rigours of apprehending smugglers as it was with some satisfaction that customs officials noted in a letter written in 1787, stating:

> There is no more smuggling tobacco carried on by vessels here now; that trade was put a stop to by our driving that notorious smuggler Knight from the Island of Barry. When his armed vessel was there, he was in such force that it was impossible to approach the island.

Despite Knight's departure, Barry Island still proved to be a magnet for smugglers. In 1788 one 'Arthur the Smuggler' seemingly took Knights place and began to give the collection officers at Cardiff a headache. There are many fanciful legends concerning William Arthur, a Gower man, and his battles with the revenue men. Whether or not Arthur's deeds were embellished or exaggerated is unclear, but Arthur was certainly a noted smuggler during his day and clearly had a reputation that proceeded him as he sought to expand his smuggling enterprise to Barry.

Customs officials it seems lost no time in venturing to prevent Arthur from taking control of Barry Island, as 'two expeditions' were launched against him. The collector, in desperation and no doubt with memories of Knight still fresh, appealed to his superiors in London for another cutter to be stationed at Penarth, and in addition for him to be provided with soldiers, asserting 'but we are confident that sixty men of light infantry are likewise wanted' and stating: 'how can the people of Neath and Swansea face Arthur without such assistance?' and 'in all probability the Island of Barry will again be inhabited by smugglers, we shall not be able to approach the place without soldiers.' As we have seen, at a time when there was no police force it was not uncommon for government officials to on occasion request such aid from professional soldiers.

More clashes between customs officials and smugglers were noted; for example, in 1788 three customs officers – Alexander Wilson and Evan Thomas and their chief assistant William Doggett – were apparently 'ill-treated' by 'the people of the island', posthumously termed by the author of the letter, Edmund Treharne, as being 'the fortress of Knight the smuggler'.

In 1791 we hear of altercations again: 'The desperate ruffians at Barry Island had a vessel on purpose for smuggling, and the name 'John of Combe' was painted on her stern. The Newport officer tried to board her, but his life was threatened.' As late as 1798 it was reported that customs officials had apprehended 'a large seizure of brandy, port wine, and silk handkerchiefs worth £1,400' on Barry Island. However, it would appear that by the turn of the century no more reports of smuggling were noted on Barry Island.

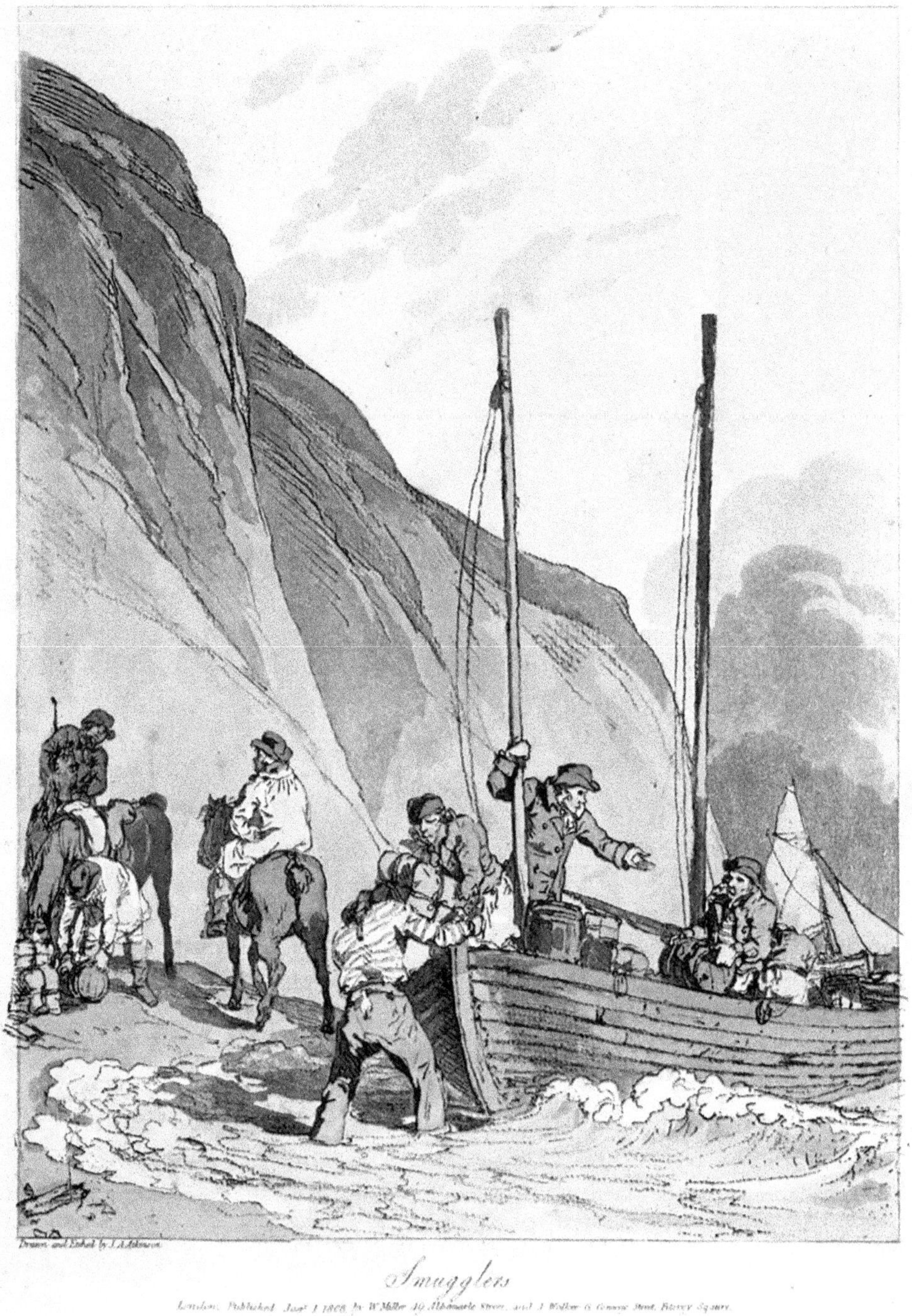

Early nineteenth-century watercolour of smugglers offloading their illicit goods. (Source: Wiki Common.)

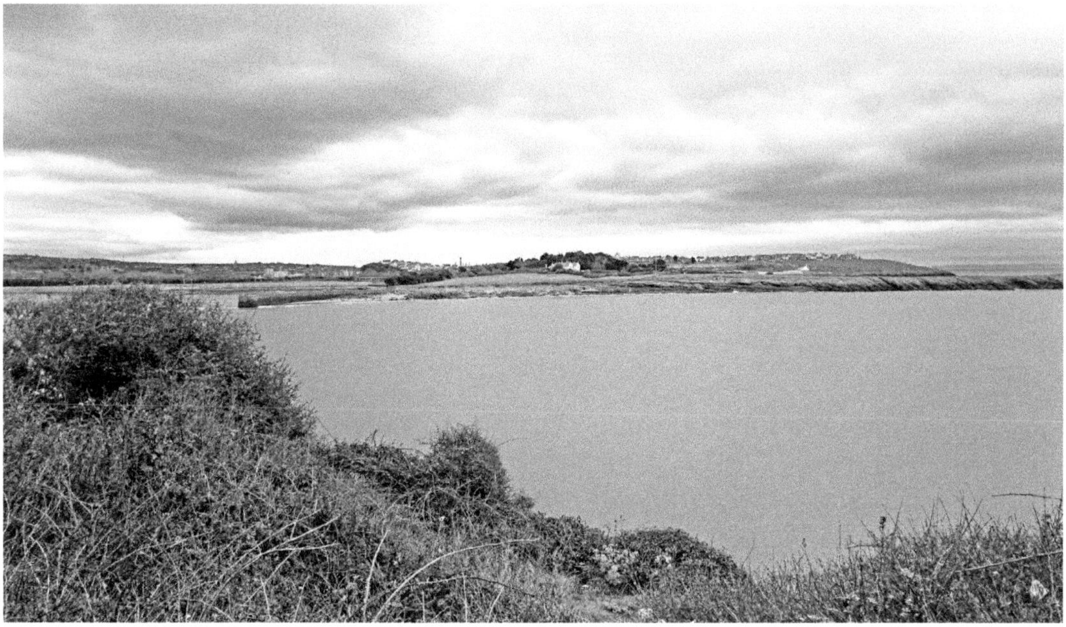

Friars Point and Victorian breakwater from the Knap.

9. Nineteenth Century

The Tourist Boom

The smugglers' exploits certainly left their mark on the local community, as tales of their deeds were widely circulated in the Barry area long after smuggling had ceased. Stories of smugglers' caves and tales of erstwhile smugglers' vaults surviving by the old farmhouse on Barry Island were well known enough to be noted by John Romilly Allen in 1873. The old farmhouse was further investigated by John Storrie, who claimed that he found no evidence of any smuggler's vaults, describing their existence as being 'wholly untrue'.

Curiously, a pistol dating to the early nineteenth century was recently uncovered on Barry Island beach, suggesting that perhaps the need for personal protection was still prevalent in the minds of many throughout the locality in the decades after the exploits of Knight and Arthur had turned into folk memory. With the dearth of smuggling, however, peace once again came to Barry Island. Evidently when Revd J. Evans wrote in 1804 he felt that the island was safe enough to visit, and declared 'the island was a good place for the procurement of conies'. He stated that 'numerous colonies of which occupy different parts of it. These are taken in quantities, and regularly sent to Bristol and other markets ... Indeed, they constitute the principal produce of the farm, which now lets for £50 per annum.'

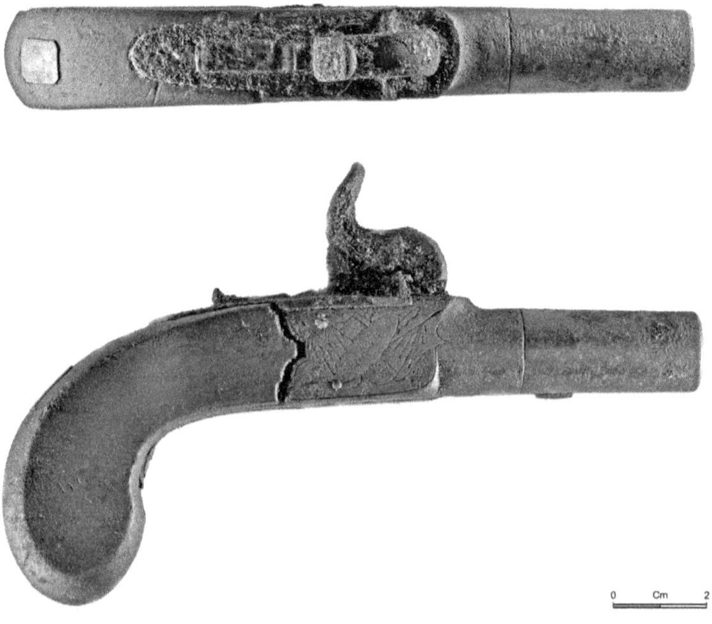

Nineteenth-century pistol recently found on Barry Island. (Source: Portable Antiquities Scheme Wales.)

The ambience and isolation that Barry Island offered conversely contributed towards the final, more peaceful, phase of the island's history: that of tourism. It seems the tenant of Barry Island Farm was onto a winning formula when he sought to provide lodgings for tourists in 1804, and although tourists were probably few during these early years, the idea had resonance. The nineteenth century was a time when tourism, in particular sea bathing, became popular. Monarchs such as George IV and Queen Victoria helped to popularise the idea of a day at the beach and sea bathing became increasingly fashionable among the middle class as the nineteenth century progressed. Modern seaside towns, such as Llandudno, Rhyl and Aberystwyth to name just a few, began to emerge in Wales around the mid-nineteenth century when the tourist boom took off in earnest.

At this point in the history of the seaside resort sublime views, a sandy beach, and ambience were the primary prerequisites for a fashionable tourist location. Barry Island, it seemed, could certainly provide these exigencies. However, the advent of the railway played a prominent role in the emergence of the seaside town, and since during the mid-nineteenth century Barry was not connected to the railway network – it was still a small village with a population of around ninety-eight people – Barry Island missed out on tourism's formative years. This is not to say that tourism was totally absent from Barry Island during this time.

Barry Island's mid-nineteenth-century owner Francis Crawshay, a prominent and eccentric local industrialist, sought to capitalise on the new-found popularity of sea bathing and tourism by establishing Barry Island's first purpose-built hotel. Constructed

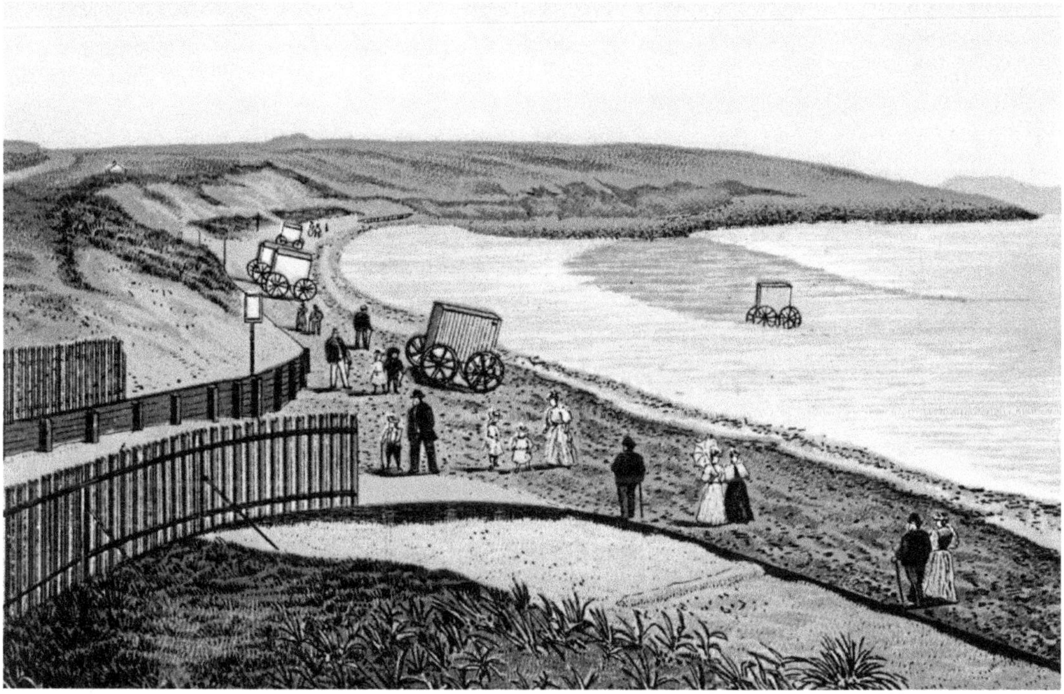

Scene of early tourism featuring bathing machines for modesty. (Source: Tom Clements.)

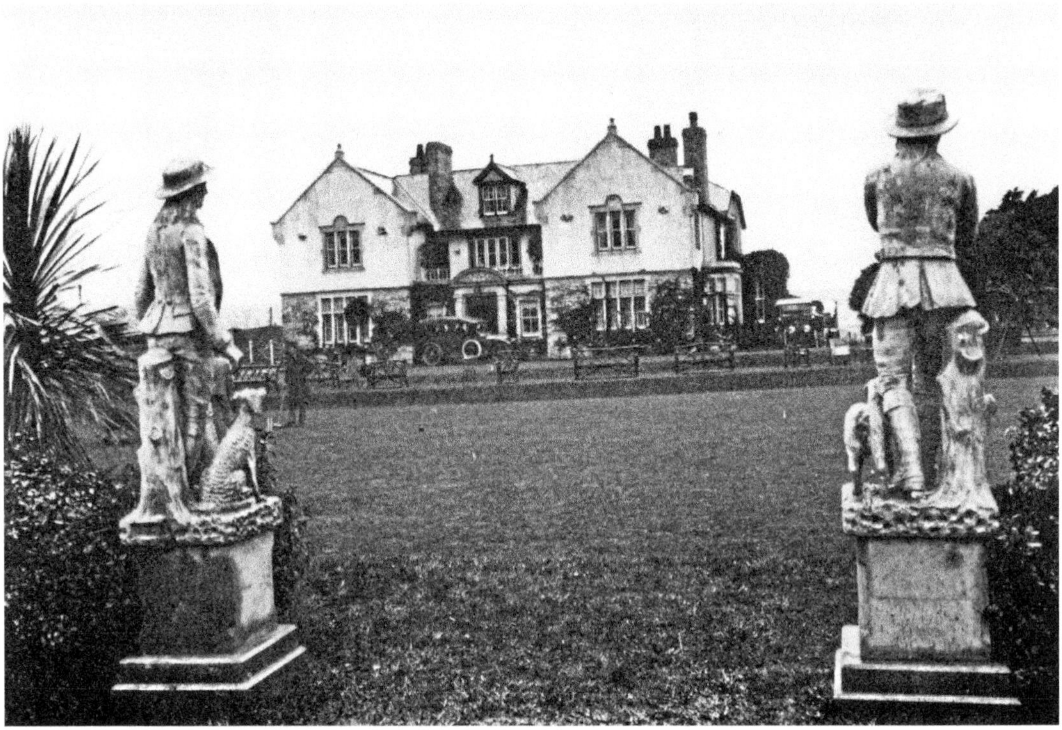

Former Marine Hotel as remodelled by Lord Windsor in 1900. (Source: Tom Clements.)

in 1858, the Marine Hotel, which was set in its own grounds on Friars Point, sought to offer accommodation for both gentlemen and 'delicate females'. This house was noted by John Romilly Allen as being only one of two houses existing on Barry Island during 1872. Tourism would seem to be the only form of economy at this time to exist on Barry Island as John Romilly Allen also notes that the old farmhouse, once used for smuggling and for what limited agrarian activities Barry Island could provide, was a desolate ruin by 1872.

DID YOU KNOW?

Francis Crawshay used the wood taken from old shipwrecks to construct the interior of the original Marine Hotel.

The Marine Hotel perhaps went a long way towards providing a congenial environment where 'the luxury and pleasurable amusements' that Revd J. Evans felt the old farmhouse lacked could be sought. Presumably business was good, as the hotel was enlarged in 1873 by the island's then owner Mr J. D. Treharne and renamed the Pier Hotel after the small pier that Mr Treharne had constructed on Friars Point in order to ferry visitors to

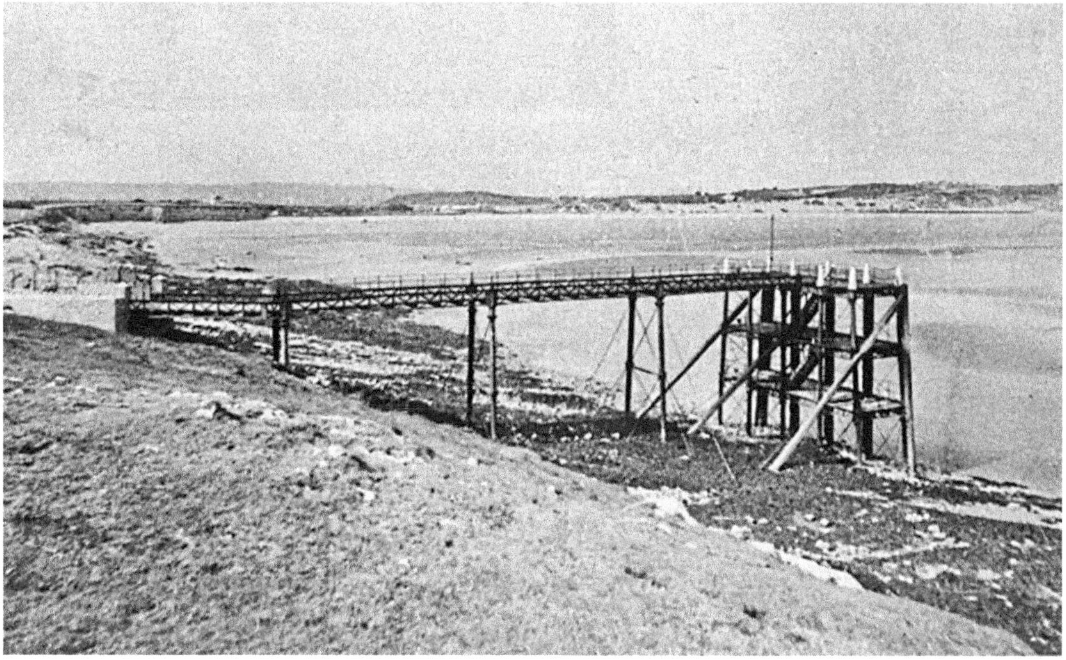

Treharne's Pier during the late nineteenth century. (Source: Tom Clements.)

the island – this pier was removed in the 1890s as it became unsafe. The whole house, however, was substantially remodelled in 1900 by its then owner Lord Windsor, who turned it into a private residence, giving it the appearance that it exhibits today.

DID YOU KNOW?

In the summer of 1876 J. D. Treharne utilised his pier to transport 12,000 day trippers to Barry Island via boat, helping Barry Island to gain momentum towards being established as a popular tourist location.

However, it would appear that by the late nineteenth century sea bathing and tourism were no longer the preserve of the middle classes and had broadened their appeal to the masses. Barry Island was fast becoming a popular seaside holiday location, but it was the presence of industry that changed the appearance of Barry Island forever.

During the nineteenth century the south Wales valleys had been transformed by the presence of coal mining from a rural backwater inhabited by the occasional pastoralist, to a place of noise, smoke, grime and industry, as the worldwide demand for Welsh coal increased. In 1834 the 2nd Marquis of Bute began to construct the first of what were to be many docks at Cardiff. The West Bute Dock was officially opened in 1839 in order to

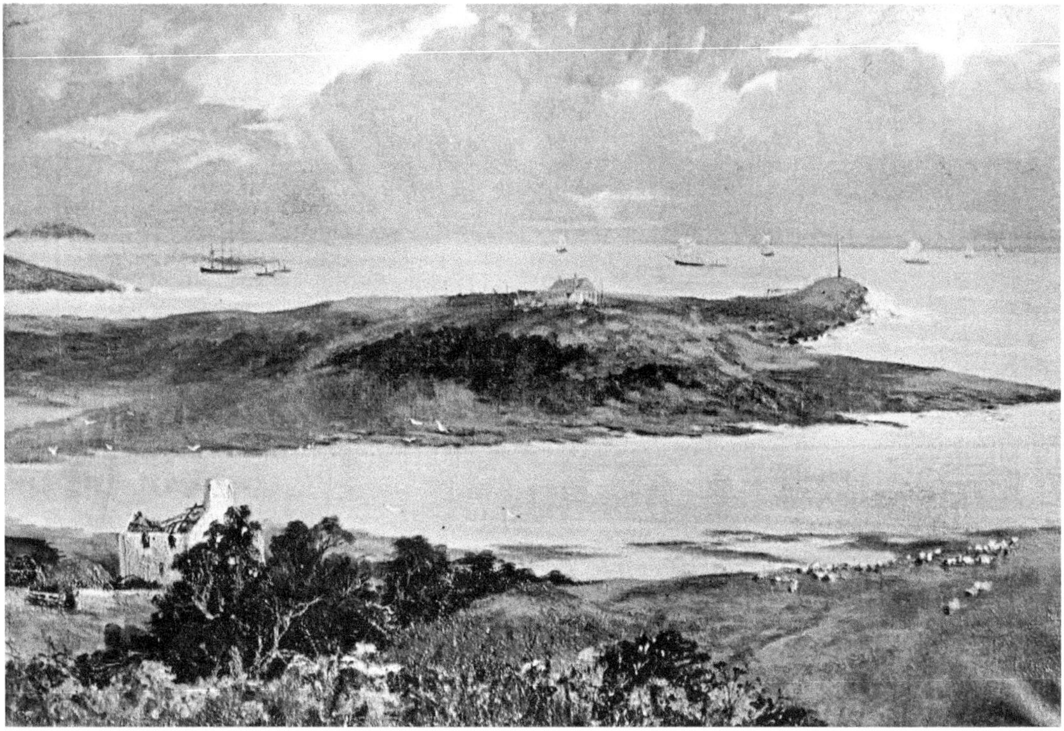

Victorian painting of Barry Island. (Source: Glamorgan Archives.)

have coal carried down from the valley coal pits by the newly opened railway lines, which had been constructed by the Taff Vale Railway during the early 1840s. These railway lines superseded the old system of canals, although they were only constructed during the late eighteenth century they had very quickly become obsolete by the fast pace of industrial change. By the mid-nineteenth century, however, it was clear that demand for Welsh coal had by far outstripped the capacity of Cardiff docks to export it. This event provided the impetus for the construction of the docks at Barry.

The construction of the docks at Barry during the latter part of the nineteenth century was a question of 'if' rather than 'when' it would happen. The antecedents to the creation of the docks at Barry is a confusing and muddled historical narrative of frustrated schemes and failed parliamentary bills based around the aspirations of rich and powerful men.

One frequent complaint from colliery owners, apart from the reviled additional charge of over 1*d* a ton for Rhondda coal owners, was the amount of time their carriages spent backed up before being loaded for shipment – to a hard-nosed Victorian capitalist, time was money.

The idea for a dock at Barry Island predates the exertions of David Davies. The potential of Barry Island as a possible site for a new dock was noted by a former resident farmer of the island in 1861, one John Thomas. The idea for a dock at Barry Island was also enthusiastically received by Captain Jenner of the nearby Wenvoe Estate, who purchased Barry Island from Francis Crawshay in 1865.

During the nineteenth century Barry Island's potential for development was also noticed at around this time by the architect J. P. Seddon, who was pre-eminent in the Gothic Revival style of architecture that the Victorians were so fond of. He formed the ephemeral Barry Island Land & Building Co., which had grand designs for the construction of houses on Barry Island. Despite some initial momentum, and for various reasons, the schemes of Thomas, Jenner and Seddon did not come to fruition. By this time, though, Barry Island was living on borrowed time.

Barry Island was purchased in 1873 by John Davies Treharne from Captain Jenner. Treharne, a Cardiff chemist and Rhondda coal merchant, as we have seen, helped stimulated early tourism to the island. Treharne also wanted to develop the island for domestic residences, which included a range of leisure facilities such as croquet lawns, a bowling green and archery butts – this didn't materialise. The Windsor estate bought the island in 1878; their main reason for this was actually to prevent a dock being constructed here that might conflict with the commercial interests at Penarth Docks (constructed in 1865), of which they had stakes.

The starting gun was fired for the final phase of a dock being constructed at Barry in 1881 when a consortium of south Wales business owners such as Archibald Hood (a Rhondda coal merchant), J. O. Riches (president of the Cardiff Chamber of Commerce), and David Davies (a company director and also a Rhondda coal merchant) wanted to challenge the ascendency of the Bute Docks at Cardiff as well as capitalise on an opportunity to significantly augment their personal fortunes. Davies agreed to provide the majority of the capital required for a new dock at Barry, although £1.25 million was still borrowed.

The owners of Barry Island at this time, the Windsor estate, despite the conflict of commercial interests of owning shares in the docks at Penarth, acquiesced and Lord

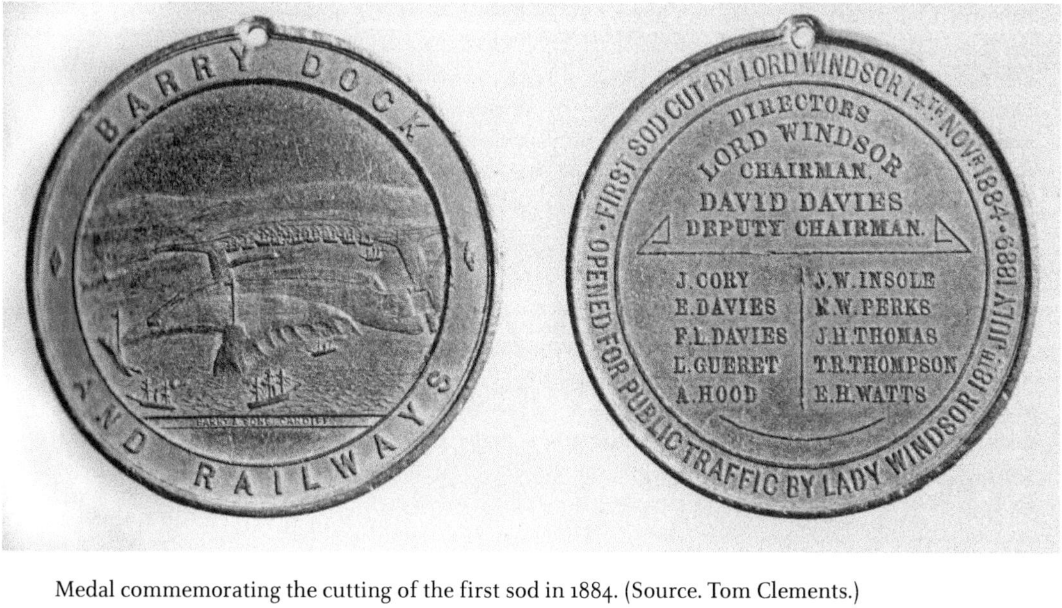

Medal commemorating the cutting of the first sod in 1884. (Source. Tom Clements.)

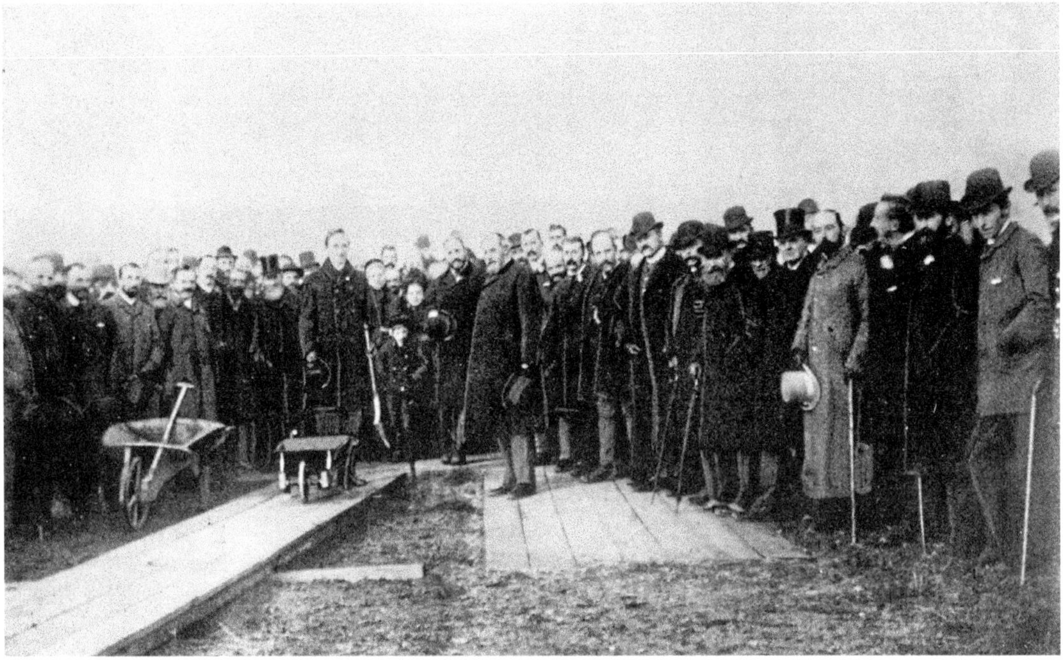

Lord Windsor cutting the first sod, 14 November 1884. (Source: Tom Clements.)

Windsor gave the consent for the construction of a docks contiguous to Barry Island. In 1883 the Barry Docks and Railways Bill was rejected at Westminster, but it was eventually passed a year later on 14 August 1884. Barry Island would forever more be an island in name and memory only. This Act also transformed the surrounding area with the small rural village of Barry and the somewhat more substantial village at Cadoxton enveloped by the ensuing quintessential rows of red-brick and stone-built late Victorian houses.

The fateful date of 18 July 1889 saw the official opening of the docks at Barry, which proceeded with much fanfare and pomp. It was attended by many persons of consequence as well as by a substantial local contingent. The first ship to enter the nascent Barry Docks was the SS *Arno*, a cargo ship. Barry Docks was an almost instant success as within half a year over 1 million tonnes of coal had been exported. This figure exponentially increased the following year in 1890 with over 3 million tonnes of Welsh coal passing through the shadow of Barry Island. For the first time in 1901 Barry Docks outdid its rival of Cardiff Docks in the tonnage of coal it exported. The amount of coal exported reached its apotheosis in 1913, where over 11 million tonnes of coal flowed down from the Rhondda mines like an obsidian-hued lava through to Barry's busy docks.

The isolation that Barry Island had once enjoyed was no more: houses were built and the fairground and amusement attractions were assembled, shaping the appearance of Barry Island into what we would recognise today – forever altering its setting and seclusion. Barry Island was transformed at a stroke.

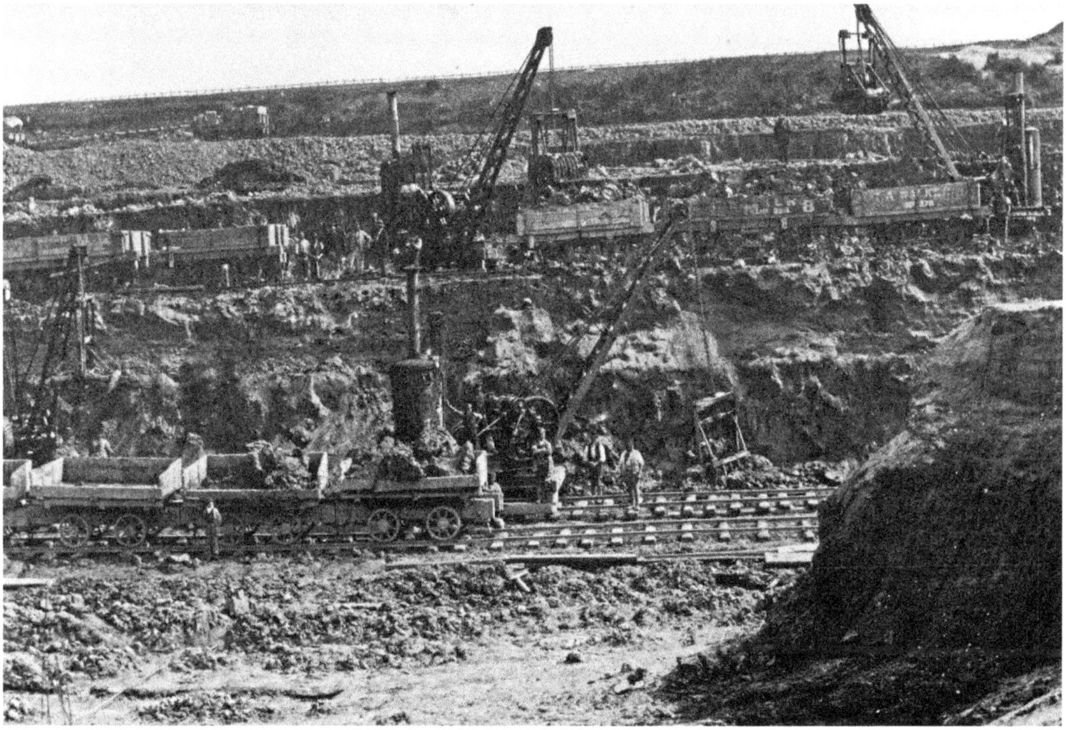

Photograph of the docks in construction. (Source: Tom Clements.)

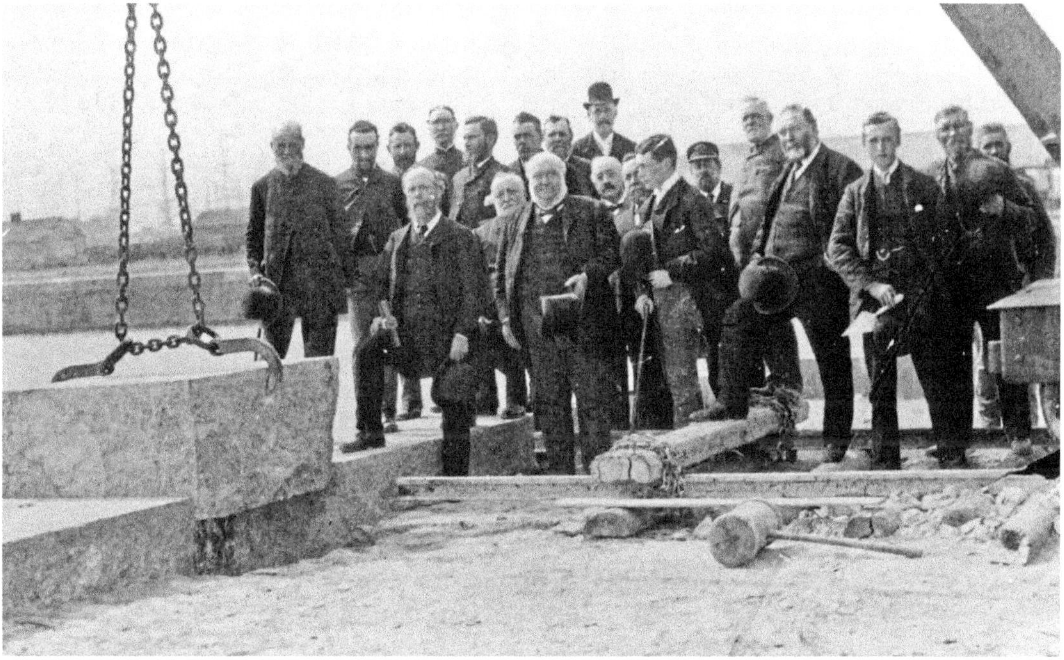

Last dock stone to be laid. (Source: Tom Clements.)

Despite Barry Island being completely transformed by modern development, there was one small strand of continuity left on the island connecting it to its distant past: the holy well dedicated to St Barruc, located on Nell's Point near St Barruc's Chapel. It was still extant during 1872 when John Romilly Allen took note of it, describing it as 'a very good well of pure water, now much overgrown with vegetation, but protected by masonry'. This well was used up until the late nineteenth century, particularly on Holy Thursday, when females went there to wash their eyes in the belief that the water helped to prevent blindness. Many pins were found at the bottom of the well when it was cleared by Storrie, as well as broken bottles and bits of rag. These discarded items represented the last remnants of the ancient customs and folk traditions that were not only particular to the communities and villages swallowed up by the development of the modern town of Barry, but were ubiquitous throughout old Glamorgan. Storrie claimed that even when the island was being developed, people still resorted to using St Barruc's Well to help cure eye aliments and other afflictions.

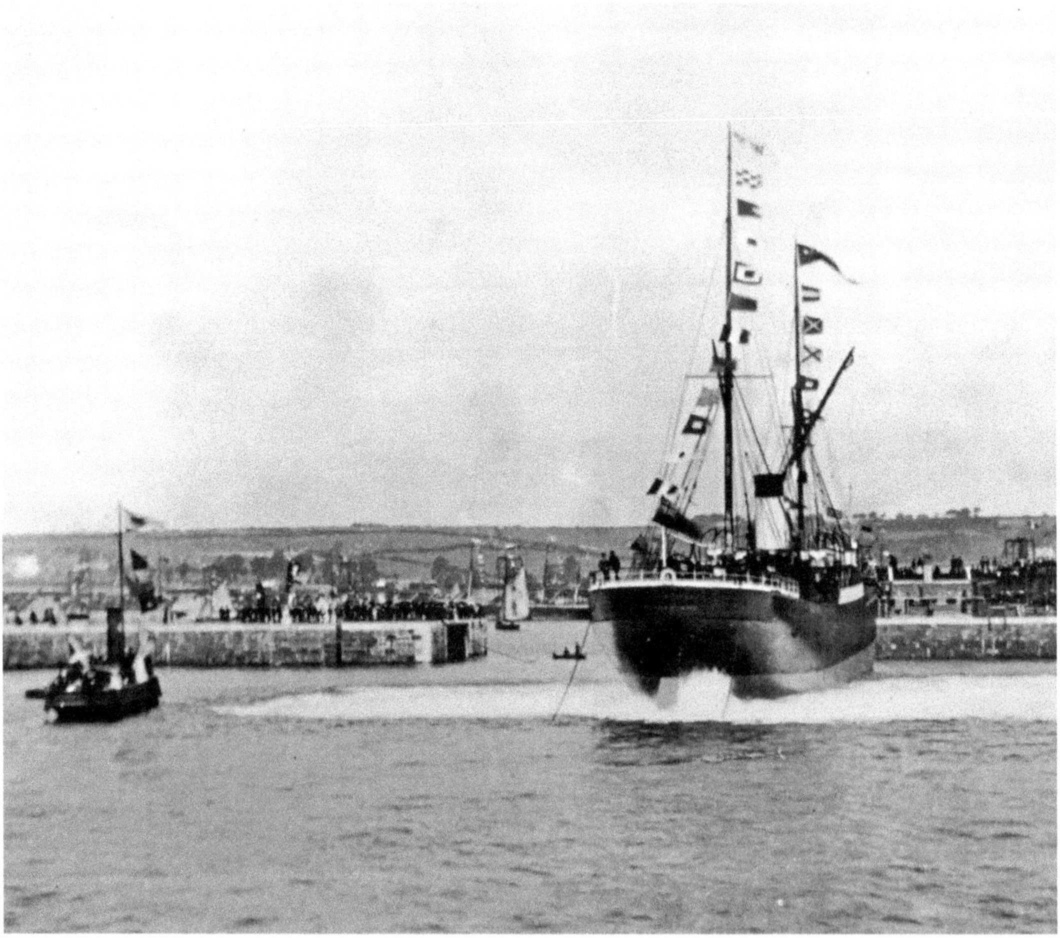

The SS *Arno* entering the docks on opening day. (Source: Tom Clements.)

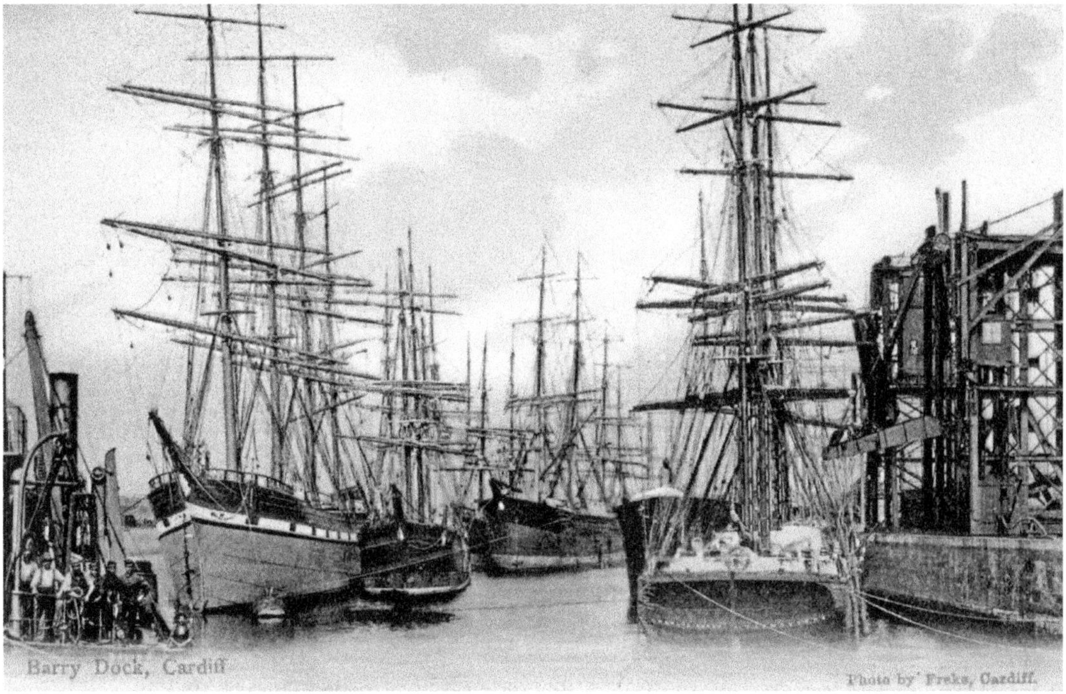

Early photograph of Barry Docks. (Source: Tom Clements.)

10. Barry Island in Pictures

Barry Island has a rich photographic history, unfortunately much more than this book could reasonably hope to include within the text. The following are old photographs that illustrate Barry Island's later historical years, including its industrial heritage as well as its location as a much loved and revered place of recreation.

With Barry Island's association with the docks and the industrialisation of not just Britain but the whole world, we are fortunate enough to be left with a wealth of early photographs of the nascent Barry Docks, to which Barry Island is inextricably linked. These range from those that document its almost monumental construction – a true feat of Victorian engineering – its day to day operation and those that are a testament to its commercial success, which typically depict congested docks full with a quaint mixture of steam and sailing ships – the old world and the new juxtaposed.

Running parallel in history to Barry Island's maritime and industrial past and probably the best visually documented historic period in its long history were the early tourism years, where everything from dense crowds of Victorian and Edwardian day trippers spread across Whitmore Bay, donkey rides, the early fairground/amusements, and shopfronts to modes

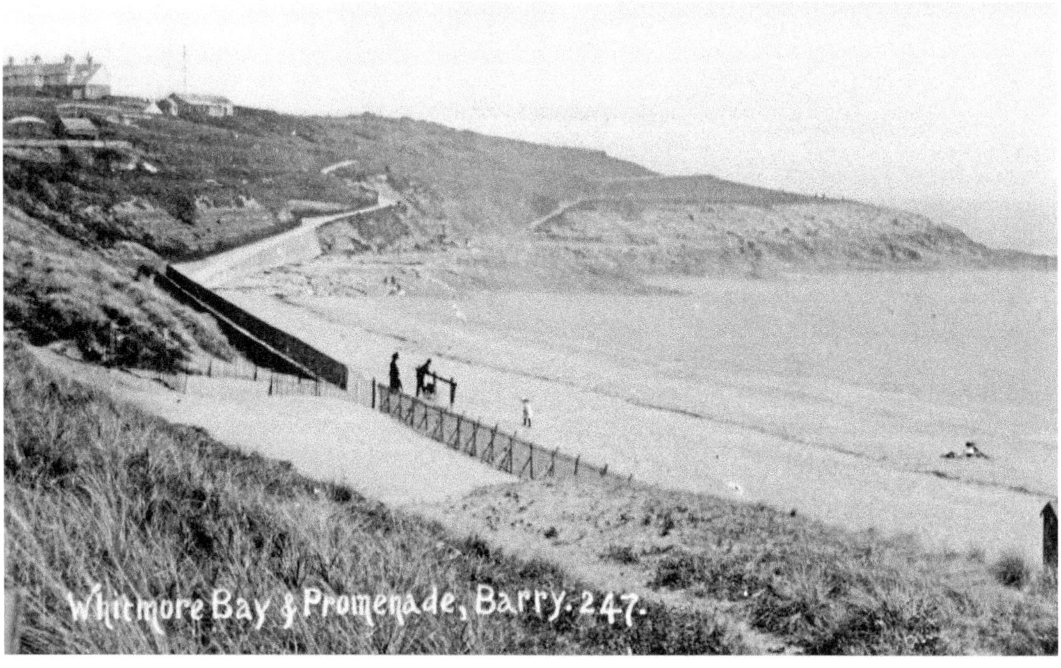

A wild-looking Barry Island before the promenade. (Source: Tom Clements.)

of transport have been documented and handed down to us in sepia or black-and-white guise. These were no doubt taken with posterity in mind and that in the present, as we visualise these happy Victorian and Edwardian people indulging in the simpler pleasures of a bygone age, we can still see the timeless appeal of a place that time and again attracts day trippers with its pleasant aspect, sweeping sandy beach and classic amusements.

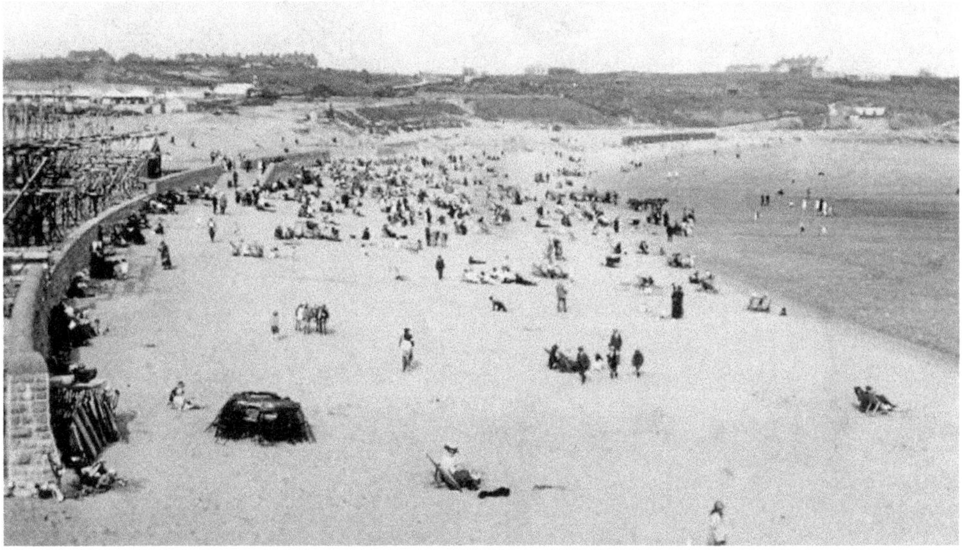

Eastern shelters being constructed in 1926. (Source: Tom Clements.)

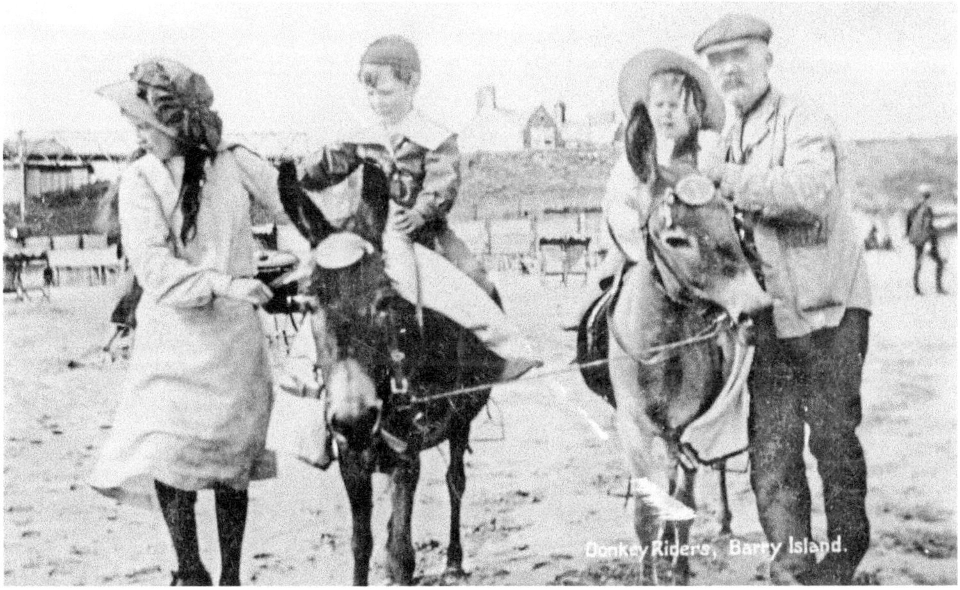

Family members enjoying donkey rides. (Source: Tom Clements.)

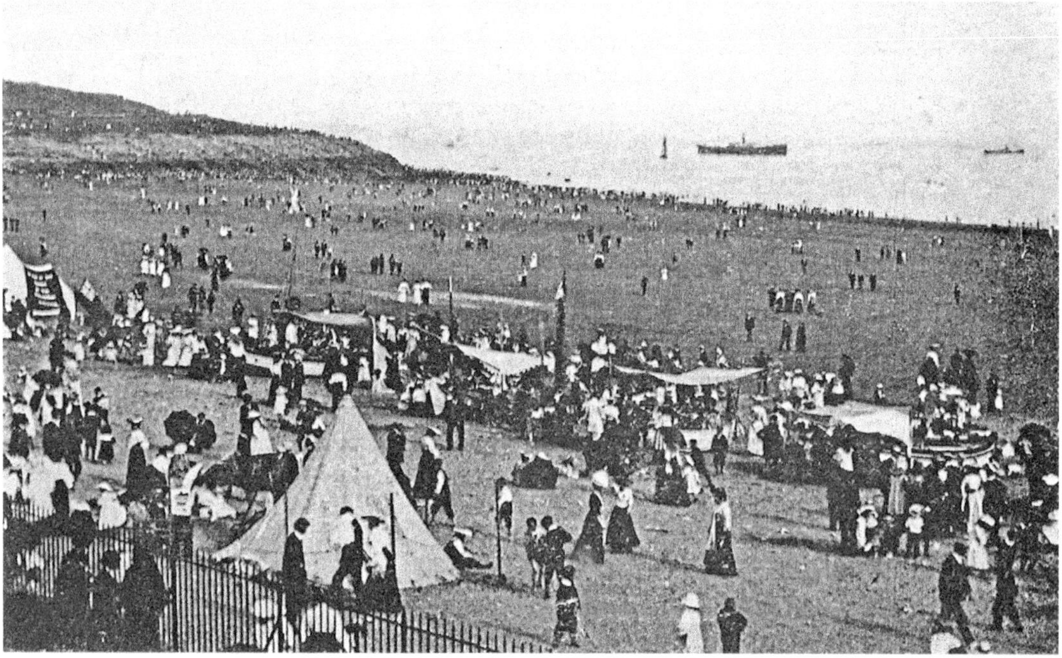

Stalls on Whitmore Bay. (Source: Tom Clements.)

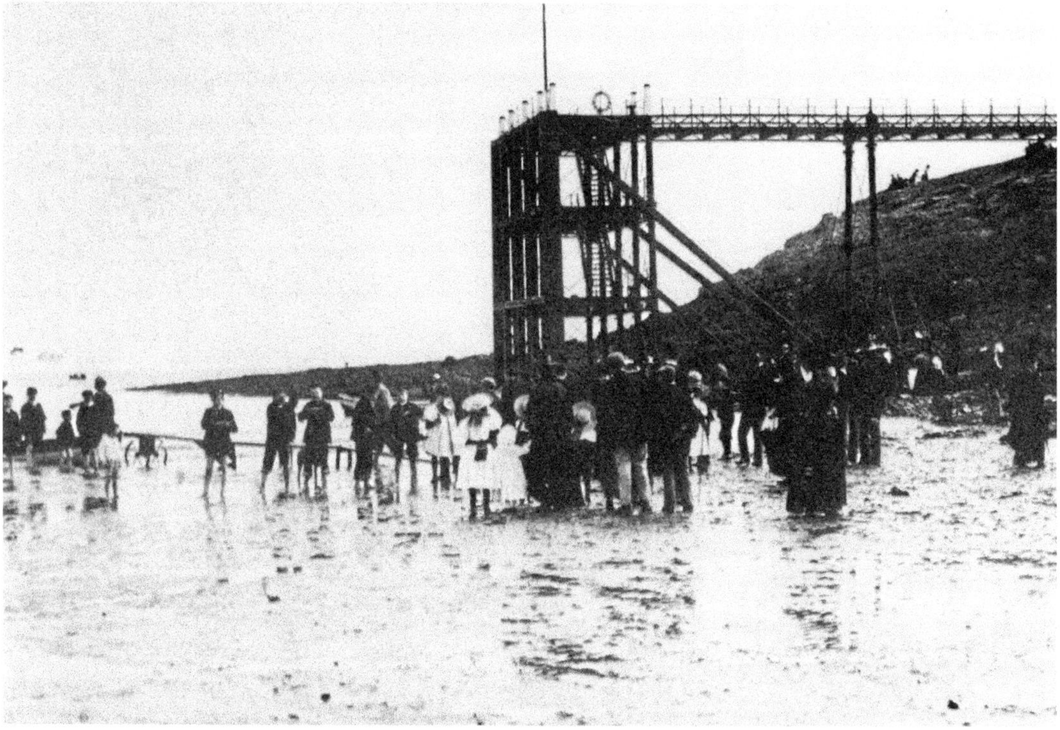

Treharne's Pier before its demolition. (Source: Tom Clements.)

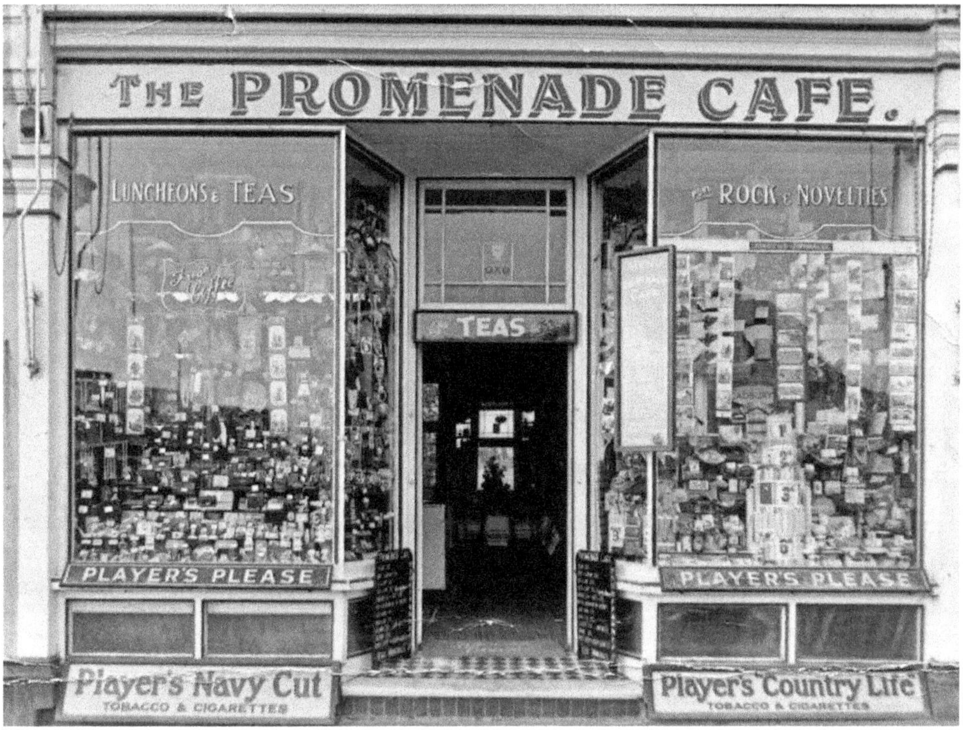

The Promenade Café, early twentieth century. (Source: Tom Clements.)

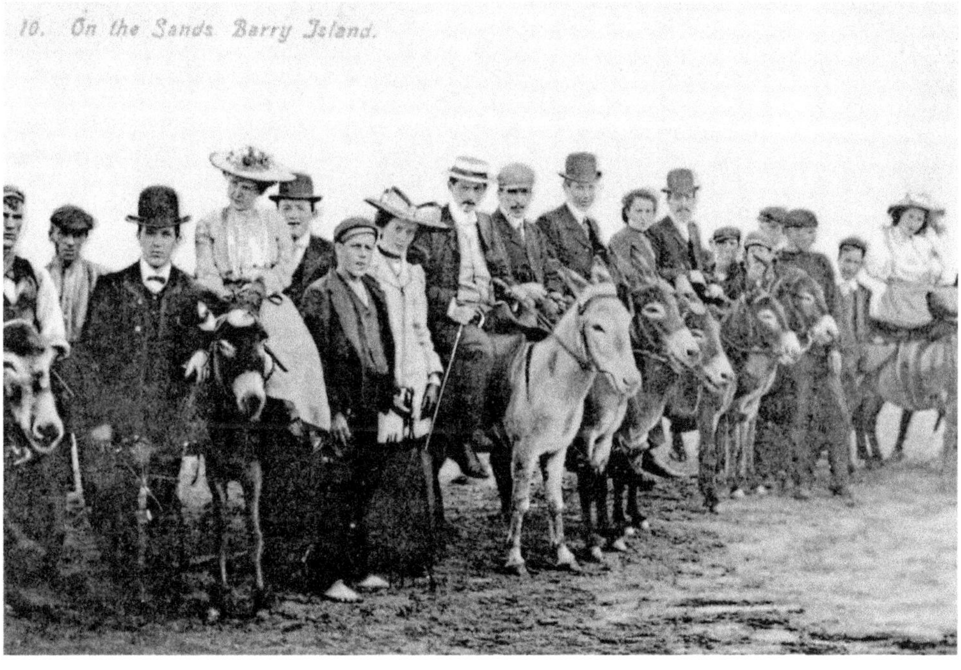

A popular attraction: donkey rides en masse, 1910. (Source: Tom Clements.)

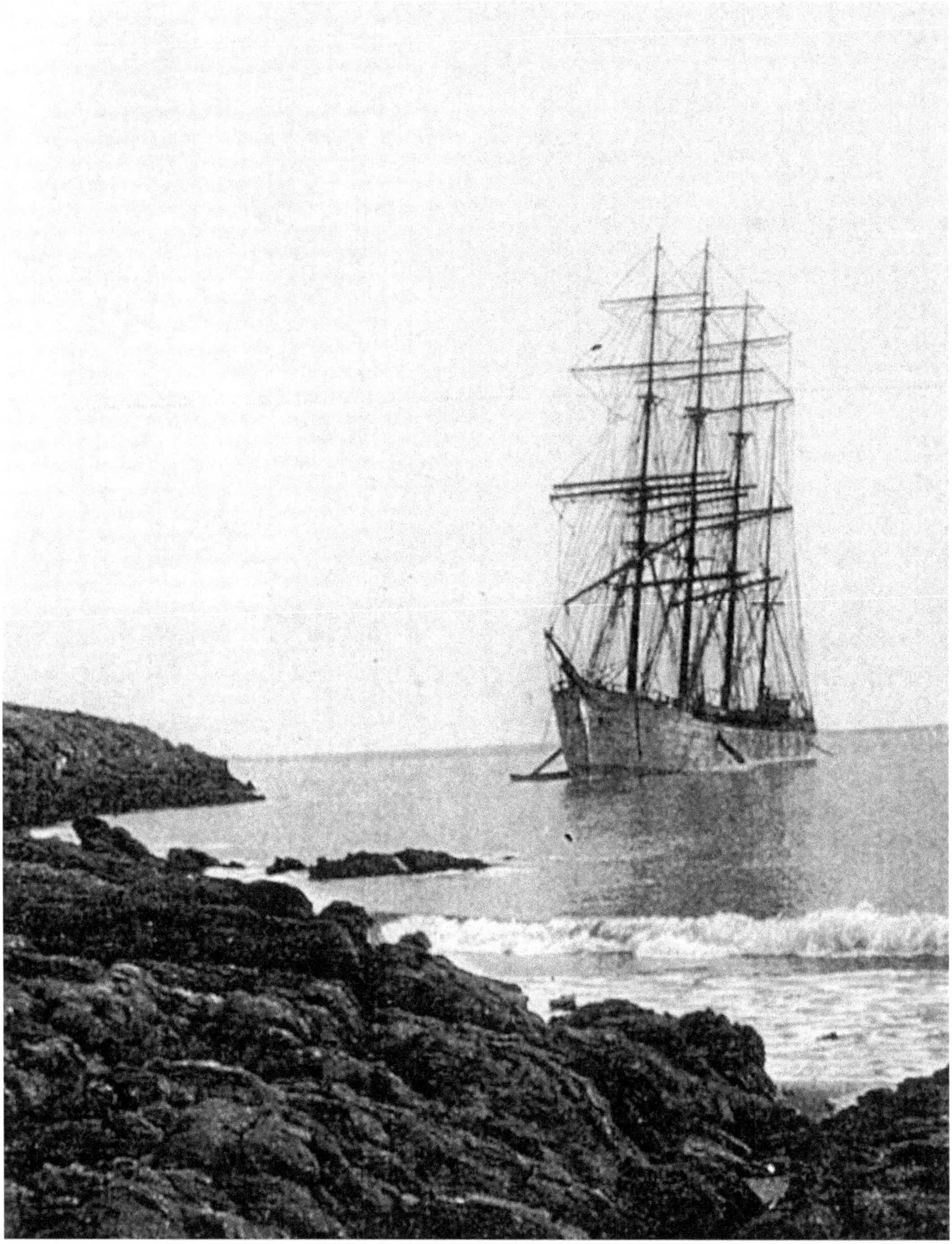

The *Vandura* on Old Harbour beach. (Source: Tom Clements.)

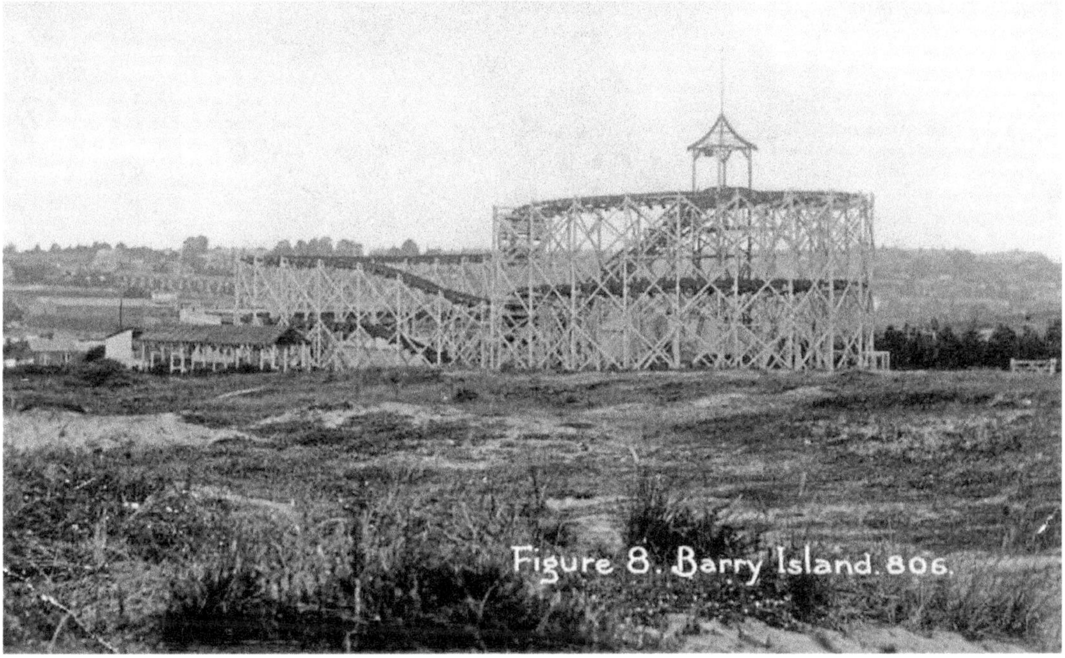

Figure of 8 fairground ride on site of medieval buildings. (Source: Tom Clements.)

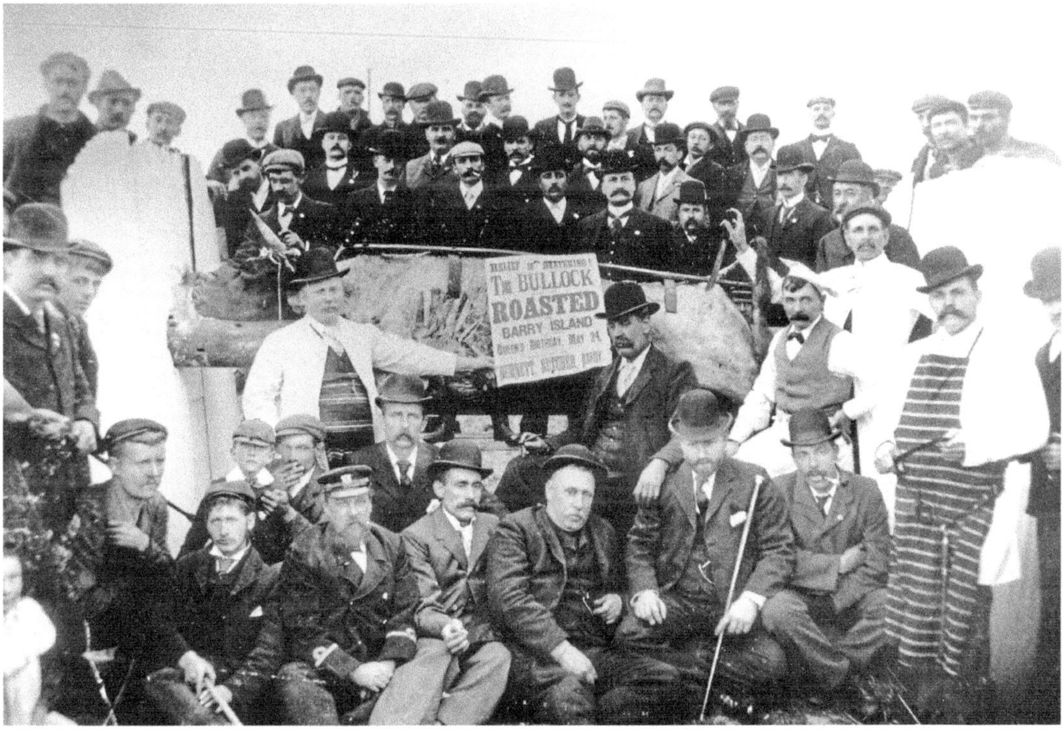

Bullock roast on Barry Island celebrating Queen Victoria's birthday. (Source: Tom Clements.)

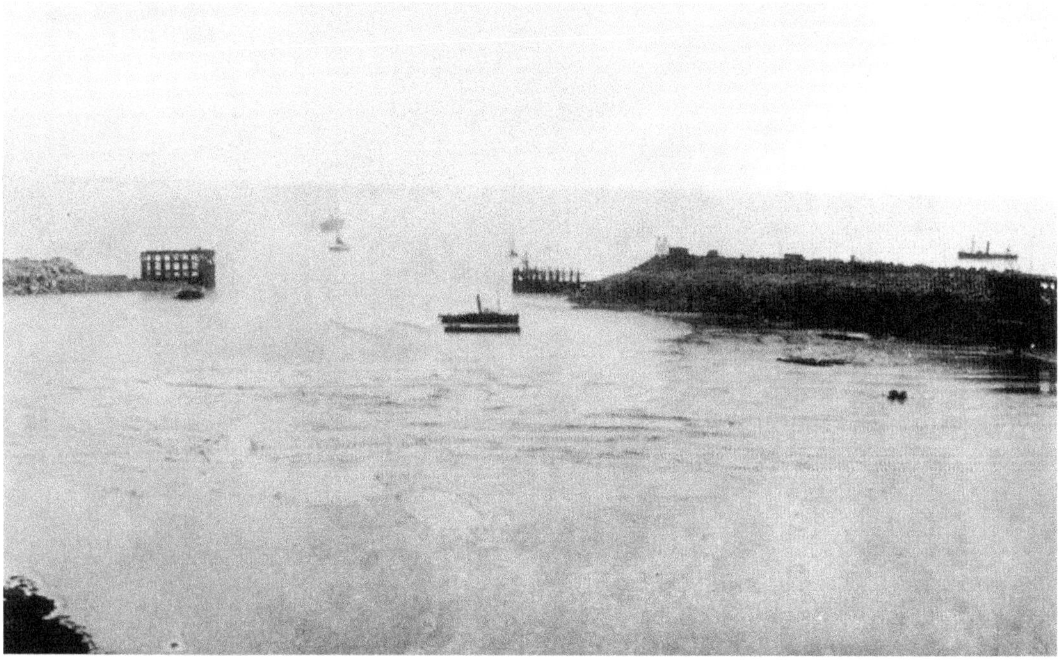

Dock entrance under construction. (Source: Tom Clements.)

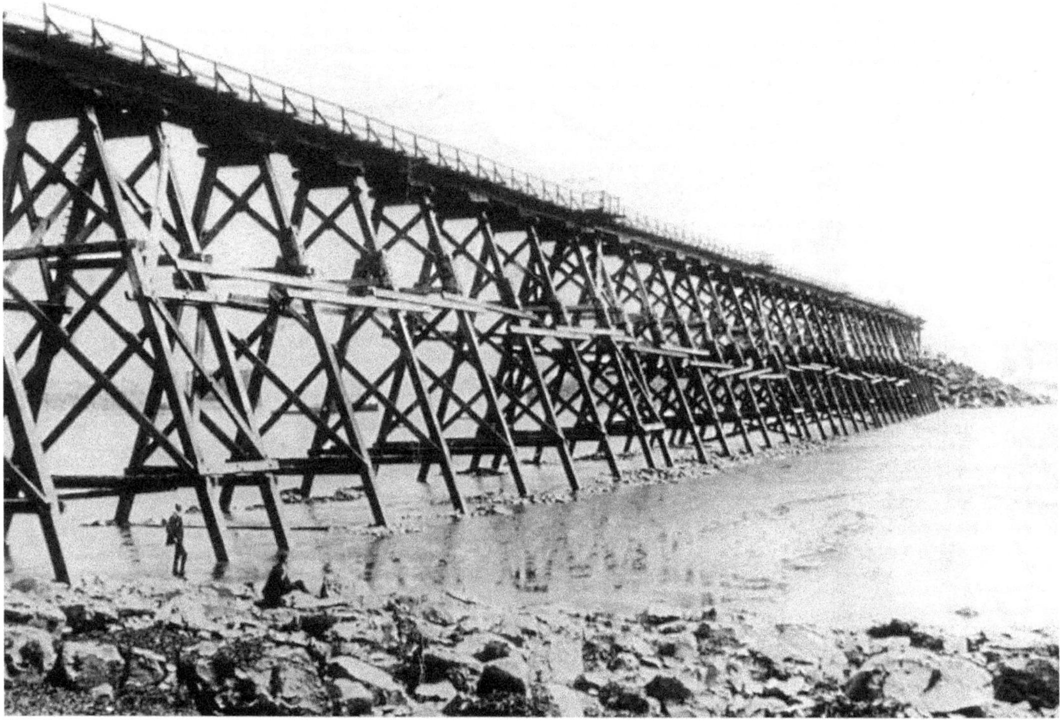

Jackson's Bay during the docks construction. (Source: Tom Clements.)

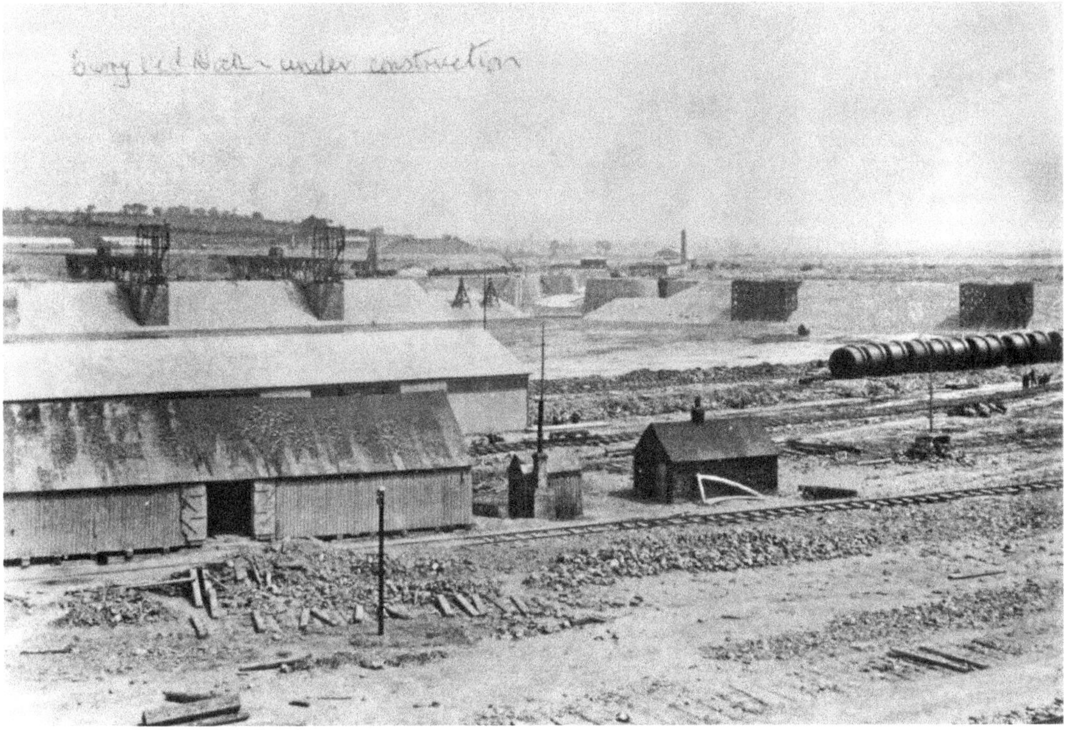

Construction of Dock No. 1. (Source: Tom Clements.)

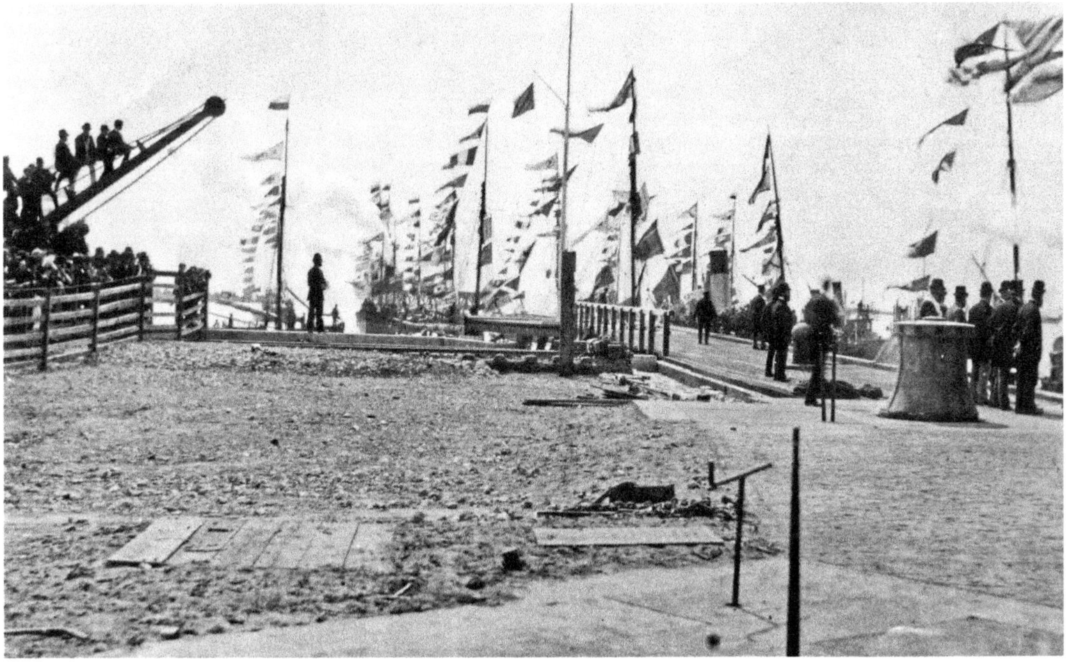

Celebrations for the opening of the docks in 1889. (Source: Tom Clements.)

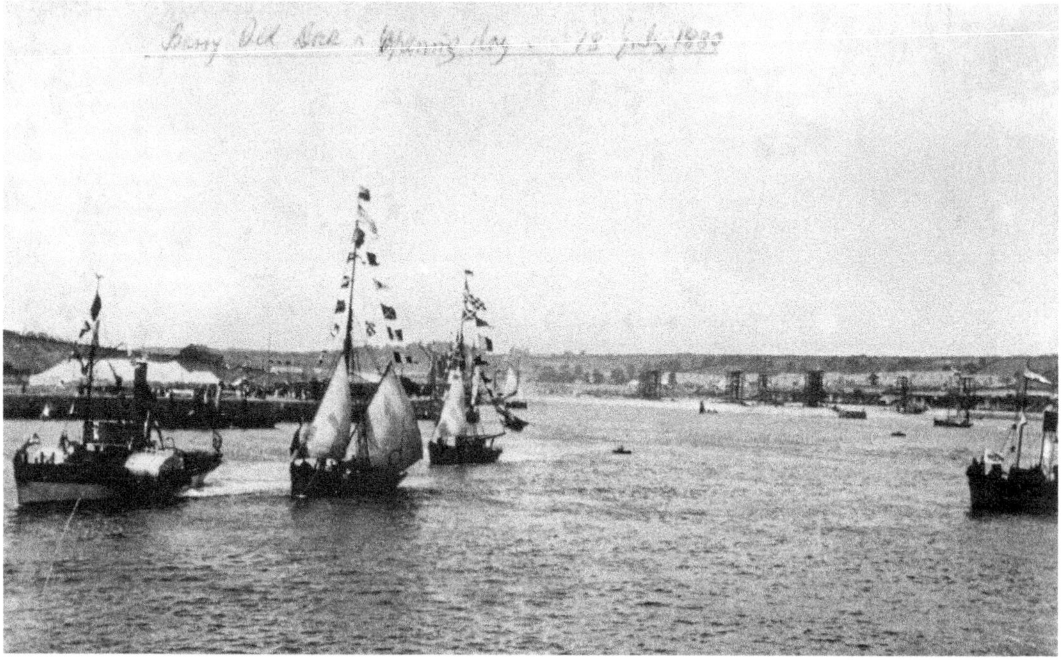

Sailing ships entering the docks during opening celebrations. (Source: Tom Clements.)

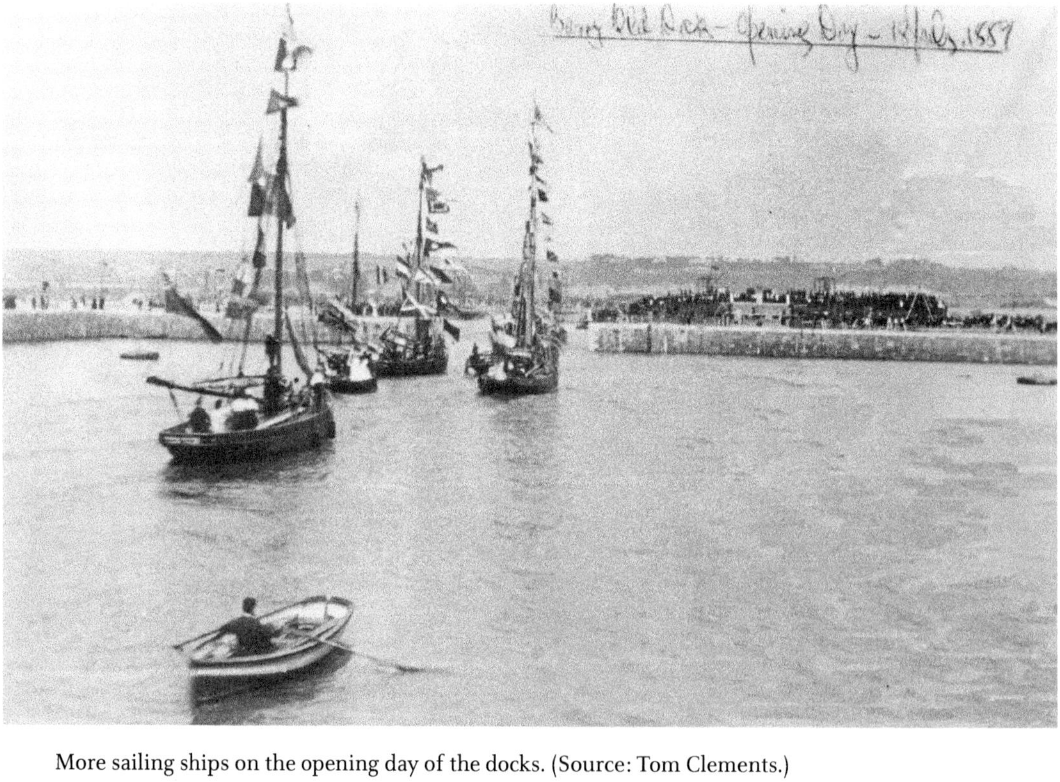

More sailing ships on the opening day of the docks. (Source: Tom Clements.)

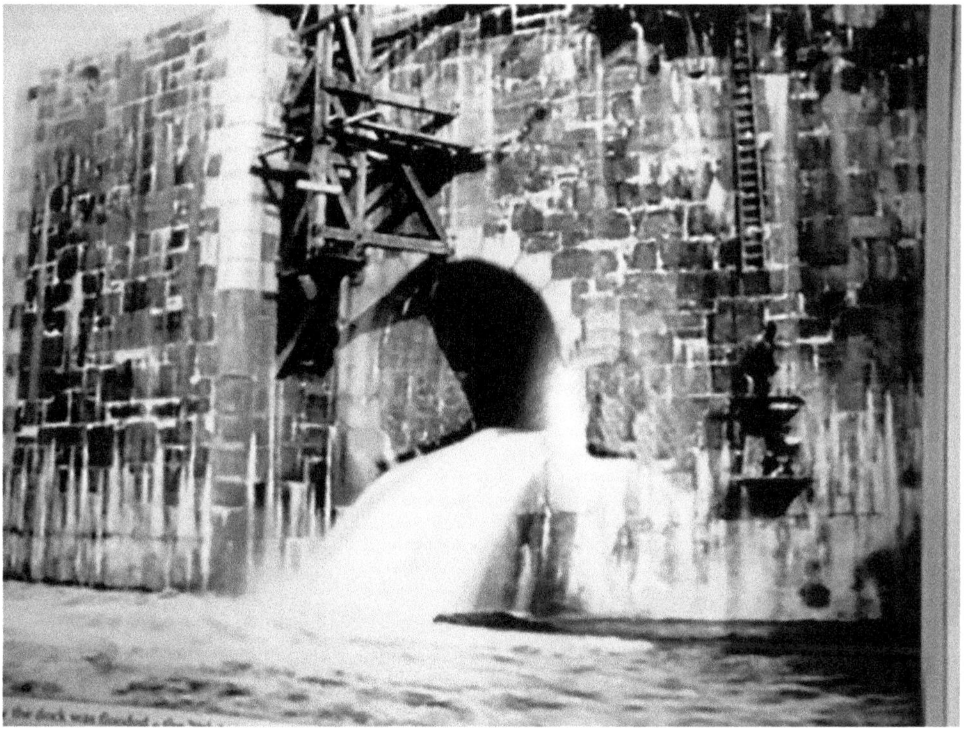

Water being let into the docks. (Source: Tom Clements.)

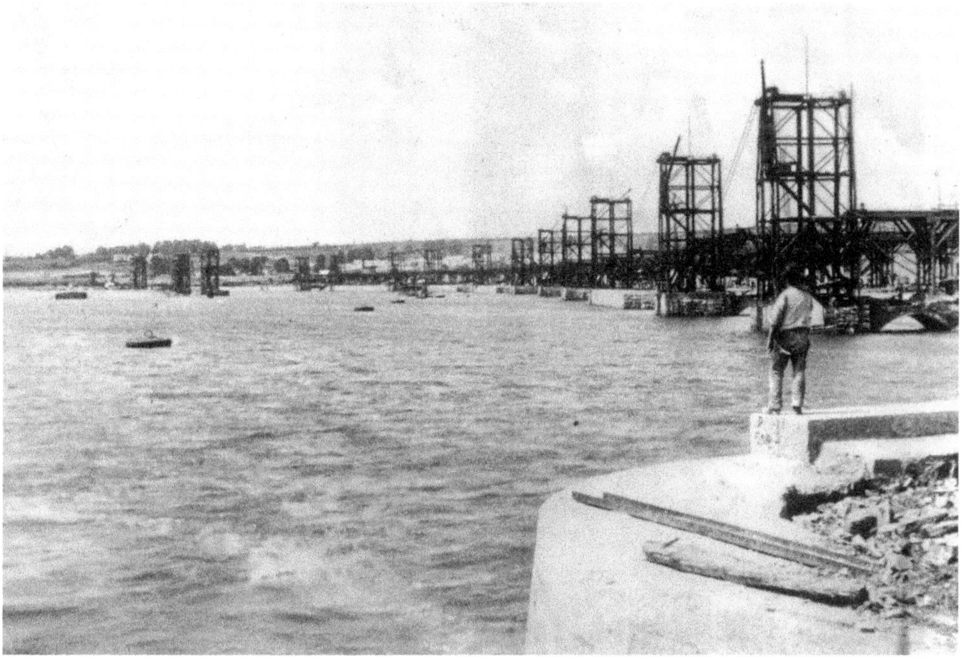

Early photograph of post-completion Barry Docks. (Source: Tom Clements.)

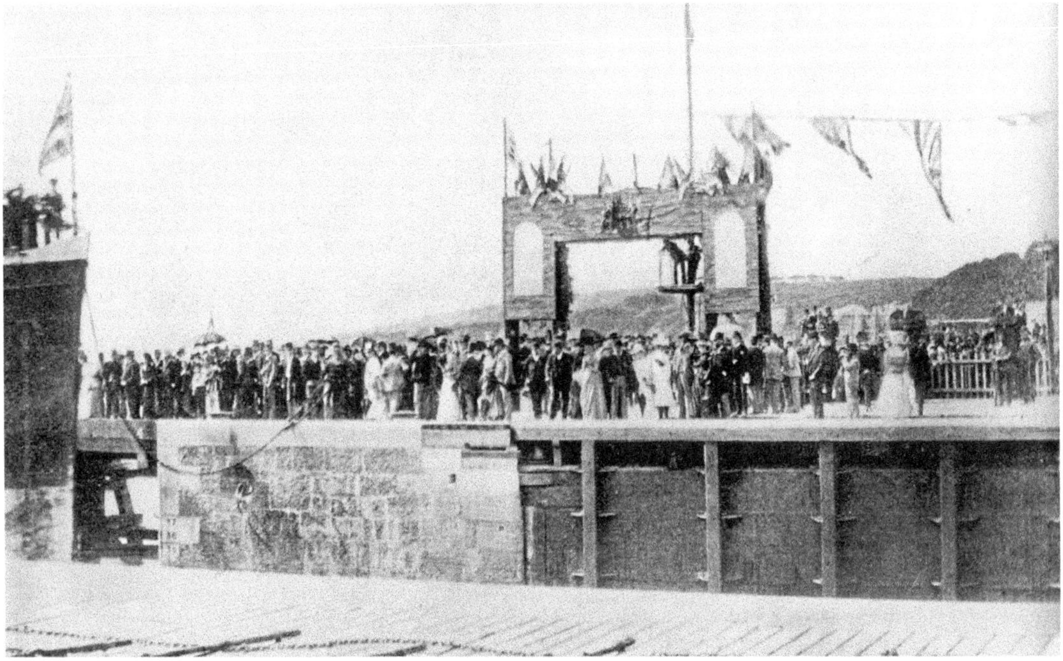

More pomp from the opening day of the docks. (Source: Tom Clements.)

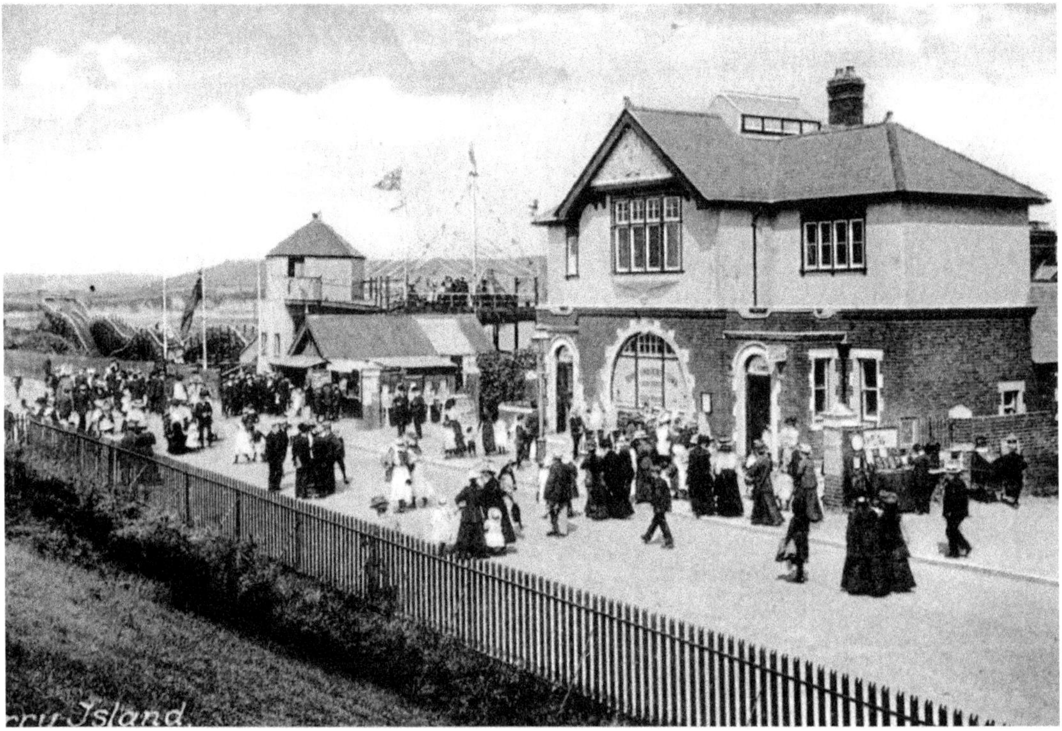

Toilets and switchback railway 1913. (Source: Tom Clements.)

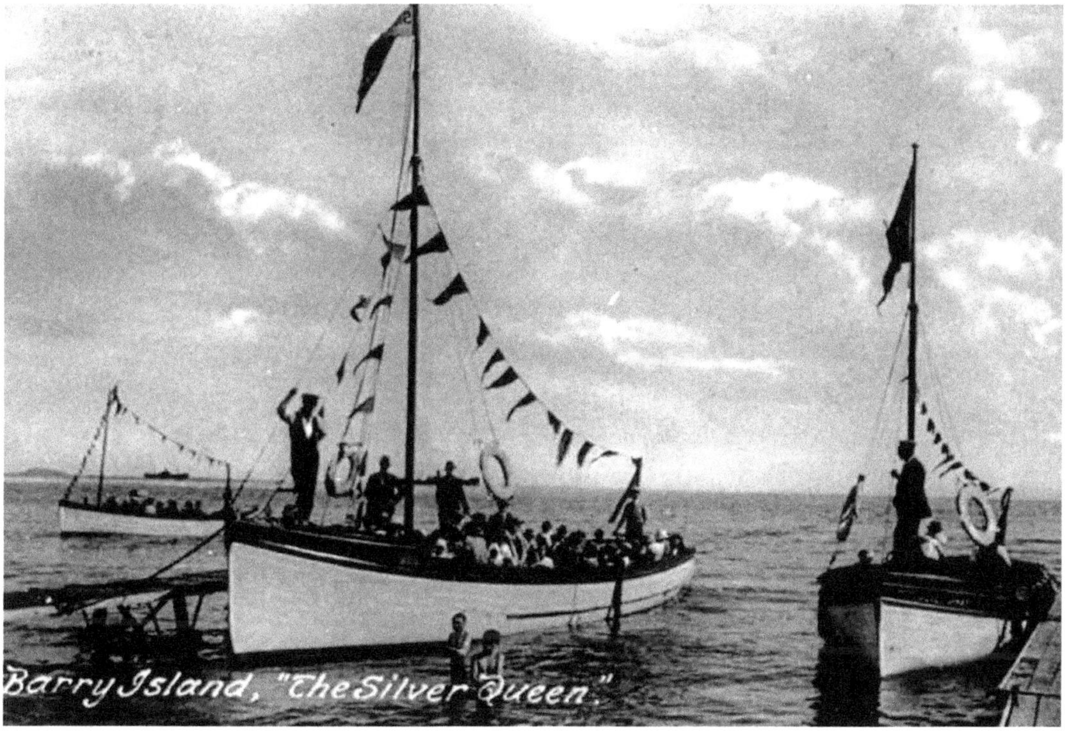

Early motor boats offering trips around the island. (Source: Tom Clements.)

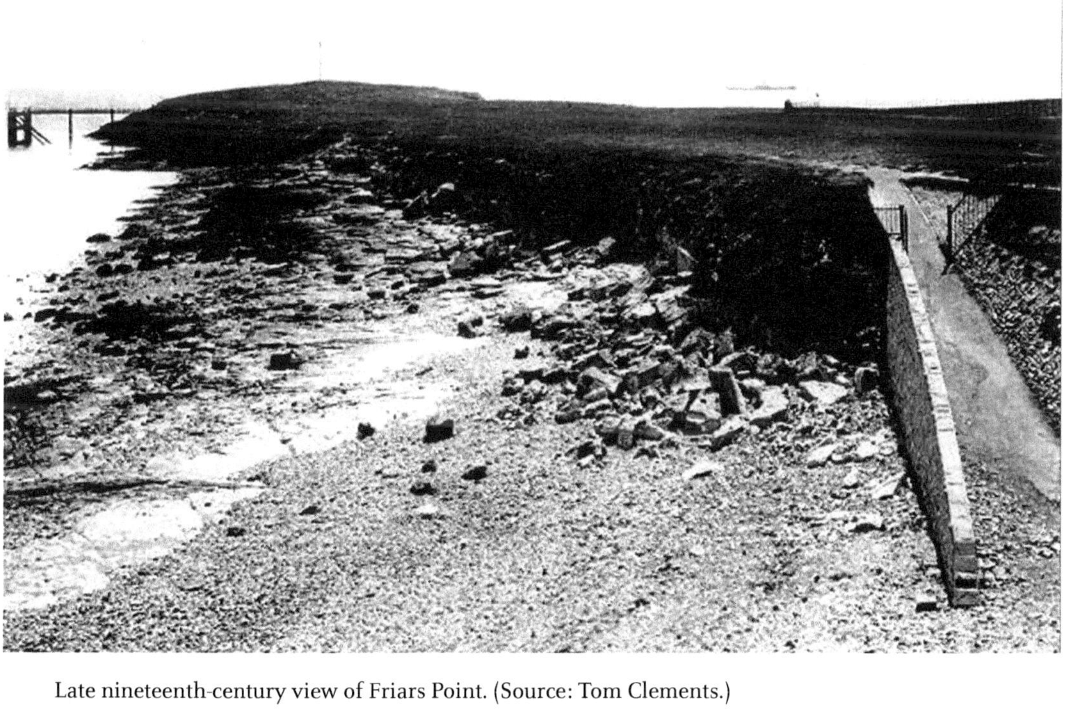

Late nineteenth-century view of Friars Point. (Source: Tom Clements.)

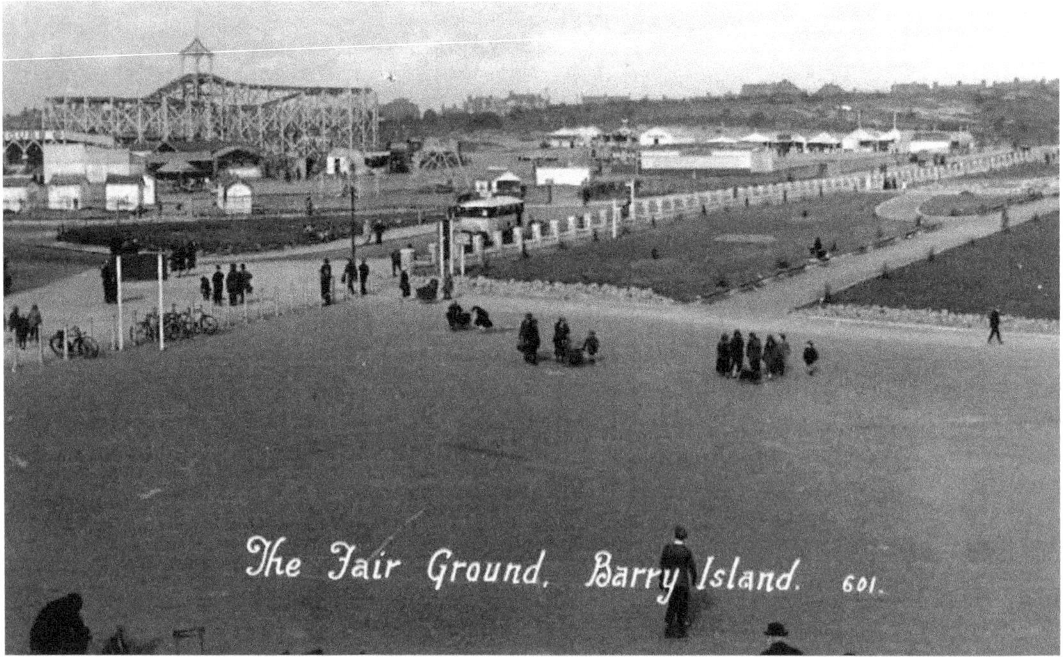

The fairground's early years with Figure of 8 ride. (Source: Tom Clements.)

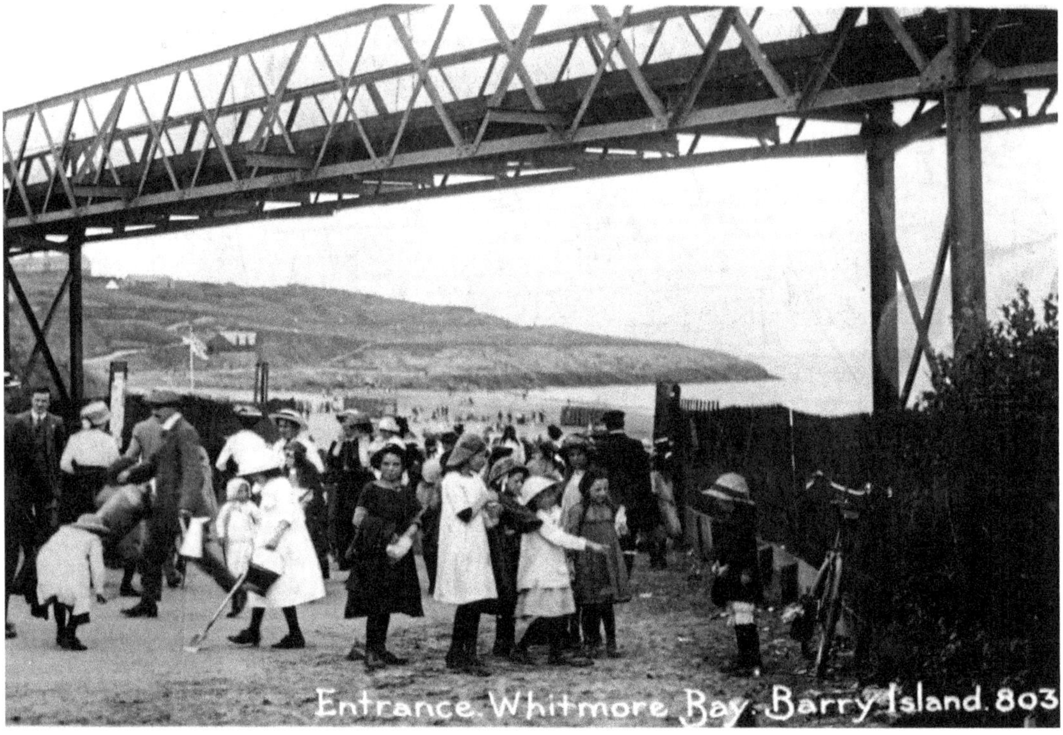

Edwardian children under the vanished promenade bridge. (Source: Tom Clements.)

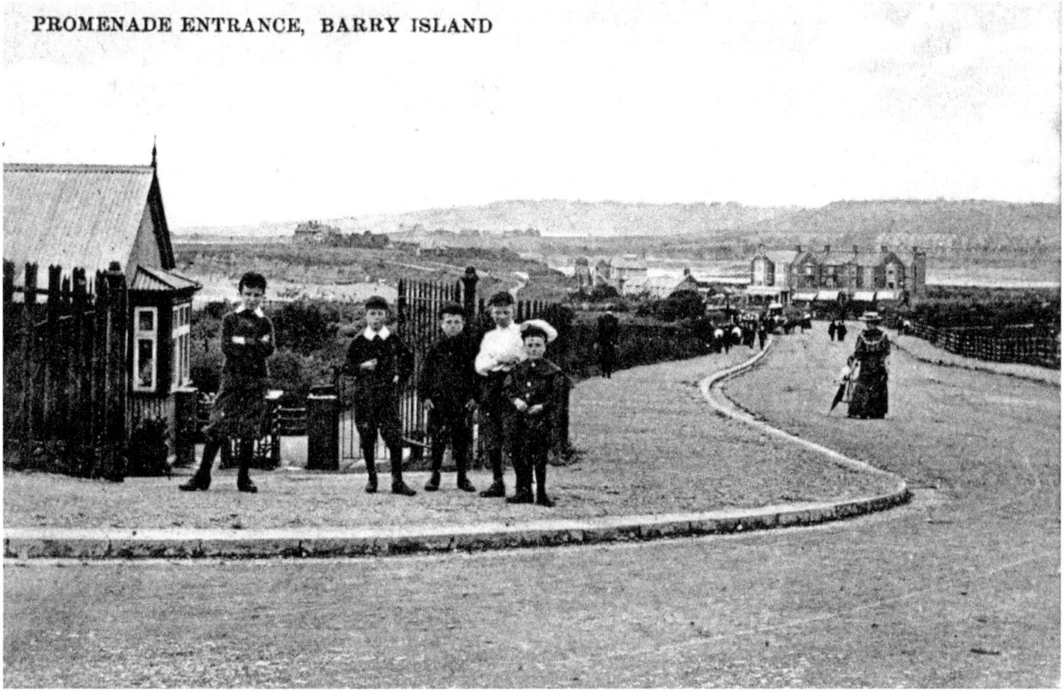

Eastern entrance to the promenade. (Source: Tom Clements.)

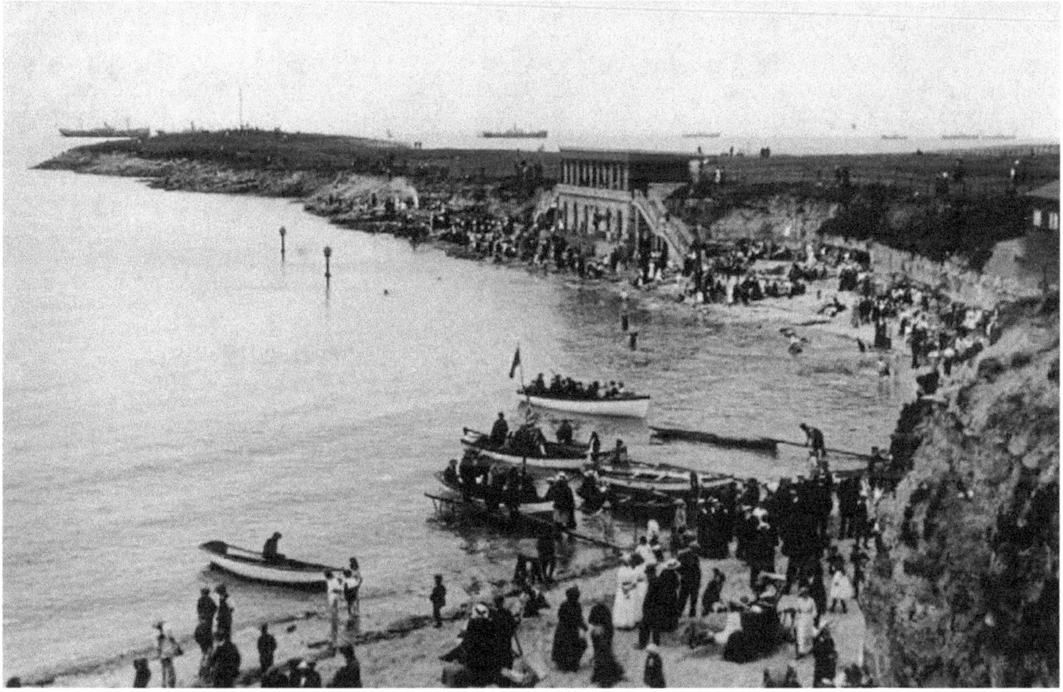

Boating at Barry Island. (Source: Tom Clements.)

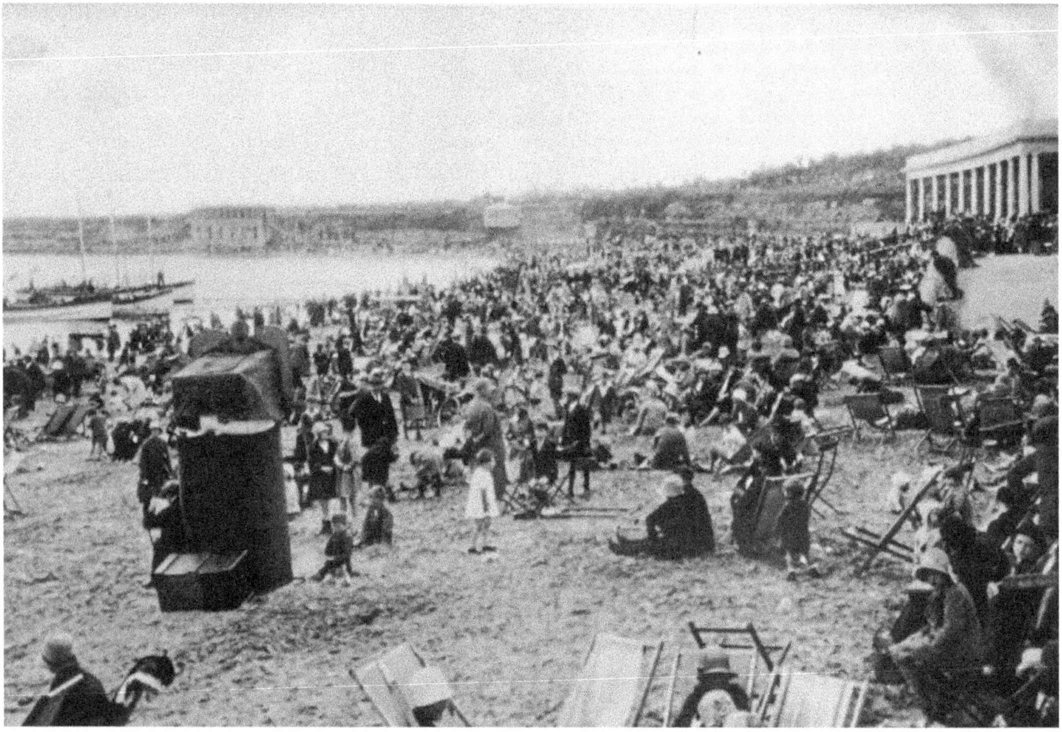

Whitmore Bay, 1932. (Source: Tom Clements.)

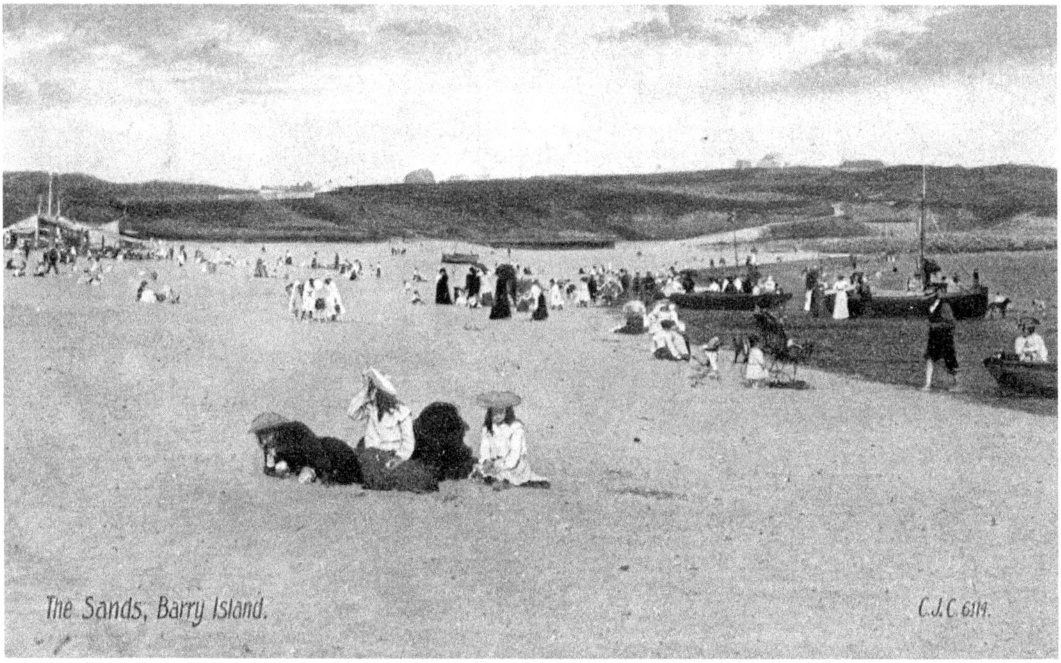

Barry Island tourism pre-development. (Source: Tom Clements.)

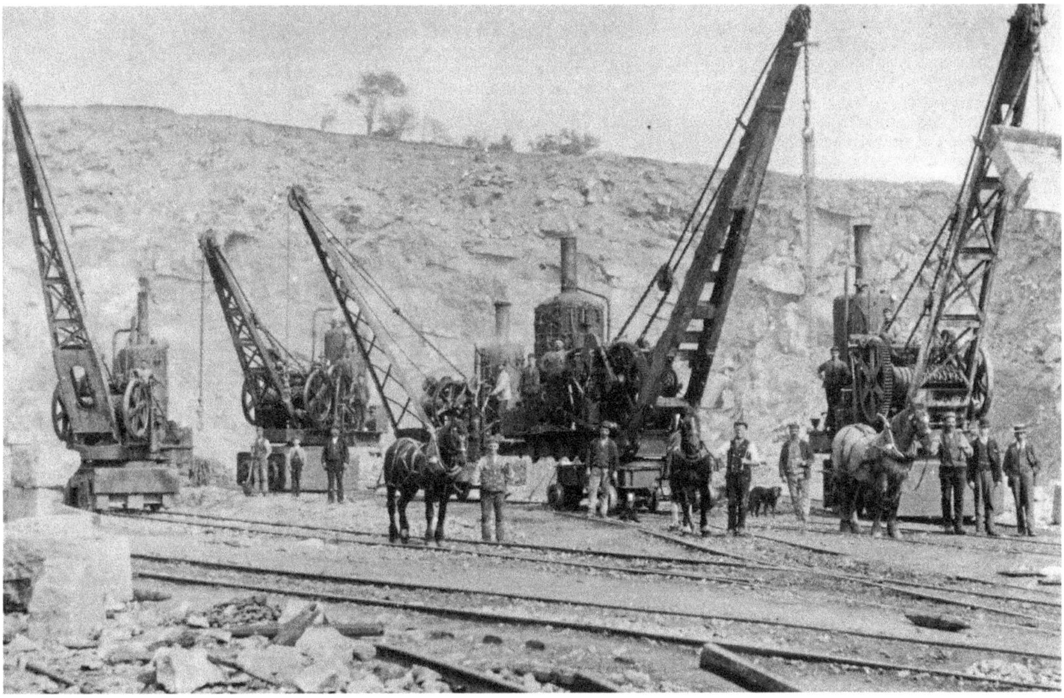

Steam-powered cranes excavating Dock No. 1. (Source: Tom Clements.)

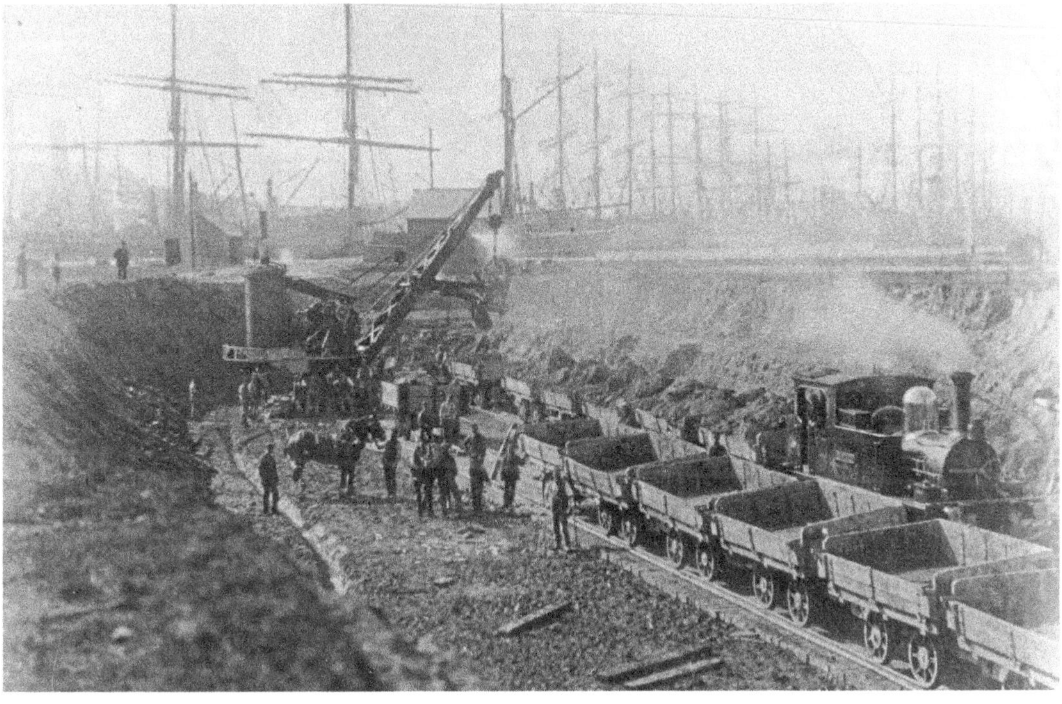

Steam and sail – construction work and ships. (Source: Tom Clements.)

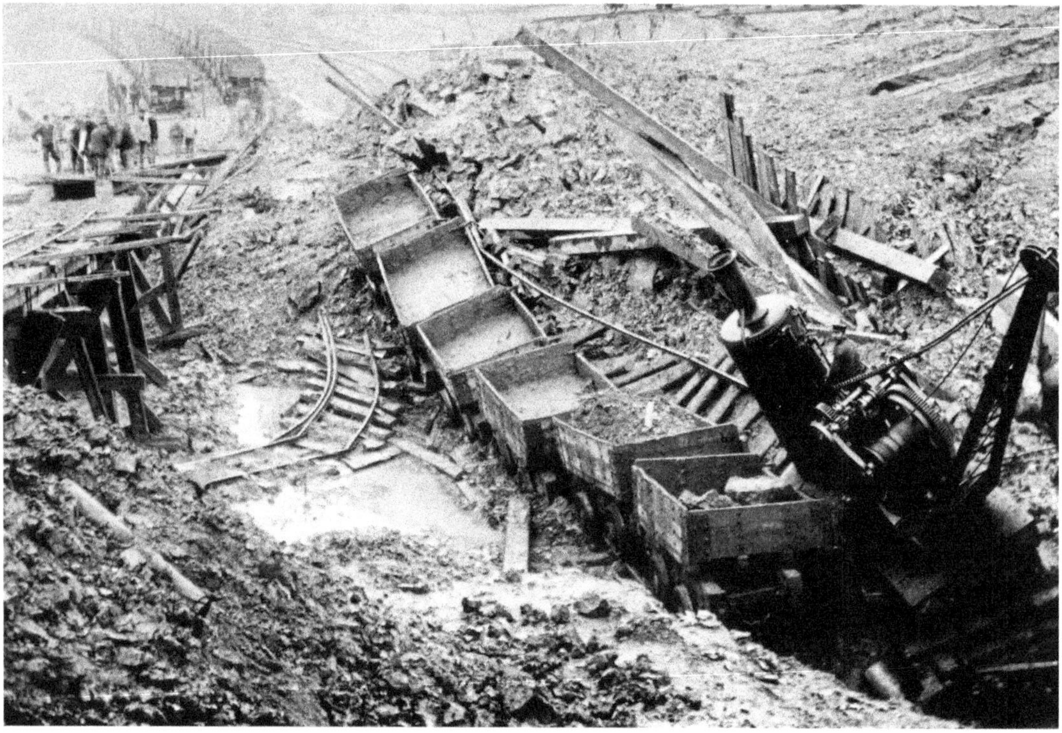

Accident at Dock No. 1. (Source: Tom Clements.)

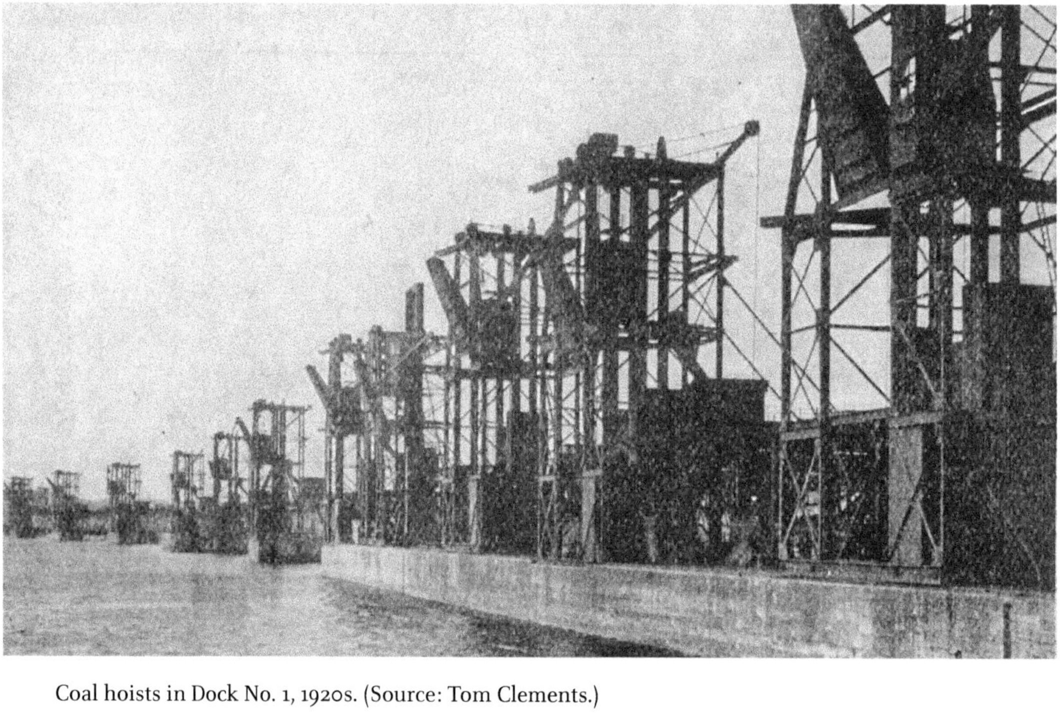

Coal hoists in Dock No. 1, 1920s. (Source: Tom Clements.)

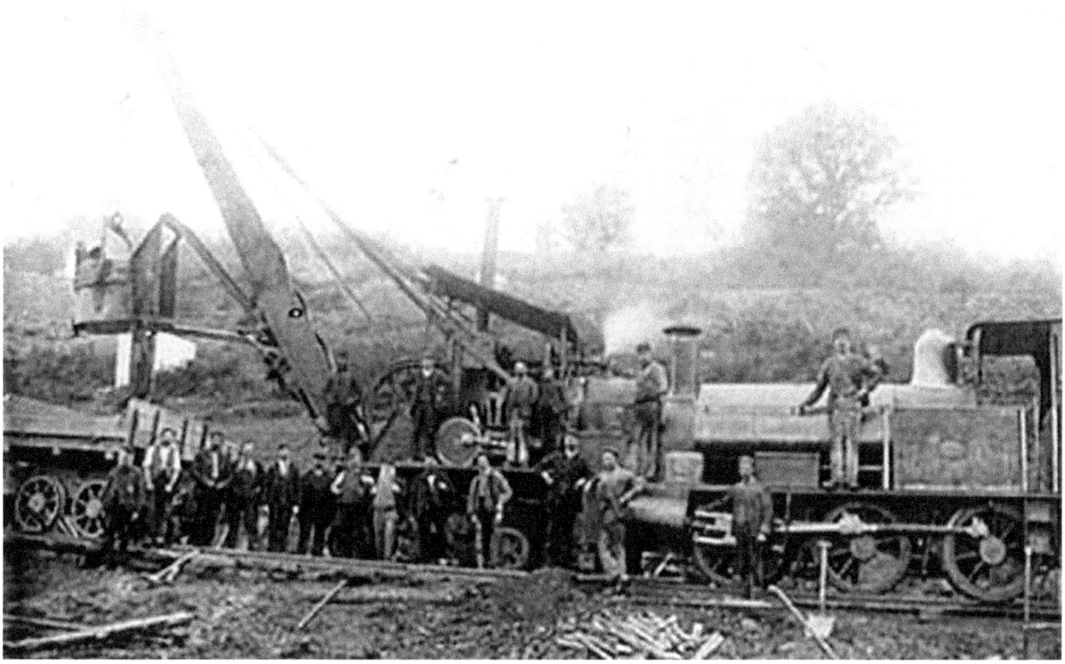

Railway construction to Barry Island. (Source: Tom Clements.)

Epilogue

Barry Island's isolated situation helped to shape and determine its use throughout the centuries. For example, during the early medieval period Barry Island had acquired a reputation as a place of special sanctity due the reverence attached to the resting place of St Barruc. Numerous islands dotted throughout the Bristol Channel such as nearby Flat Holm and Steep Holm, as well as further away Caldey Island, also have close associations with the lives of the early saints and reputations as places of religious sanctity. Many of these islands also contain later medieval religious establishments. During the eighteenth century there was perhaps no island in the Bristol Channel that was not frequented by smugglers and pirates, all of which have cultivated their own colourful legends and stories about the freebooters who plied their illicit trade therein.

Barry Island's history, therefore, seems reflective of the wider events that occurred throughout south Wales and beyond. However, whereas Flat Holm, for example, has retained its quiet solitude and status as an island, Barry Island has been transformed by modern development. The era of industry in south Wales and the need for relaxation and leisure time for the working classes redefined Barry Island from an isolated backwater that was the haunt of pilgrims and smugglers, to a thriving place of fun and leisure. Indeed, this is the general impression most people have of Barry Island in the consciousness of those who remember it fondly as a busy holiday destination, a far cry from a place 'that inspires melancholy', as Revd J. Evans saw fit to describe it in his visit of 1804. If we consider, however, that the docks had not been constructed, not only would the pastoral, sleepy rural ambience of old Barry village and its hinterland perhaps been preserved but Barry Island, in all probability, would still be an island.

DID YOU KNOW?

St Barruc's Chapel is still consecrated ground and is used occasionally for religious ceremonies. Also the modern church of St Barruc's, which is contiguous to the old site, is the only church in the world dedicated to this saint.

Despite the fact that tourism has waned within the last few decades, the sandy beaches of Whitmore Bay, and to a lesser extent Jackson's Bay and Watchtower Bay, still exhibit universal appeal and are popular with both locals and tourists during the summer months, and will probably always continue to exert their appeal to those who crave sun, sea and sand. During the last few years Barry Island has been subject to a

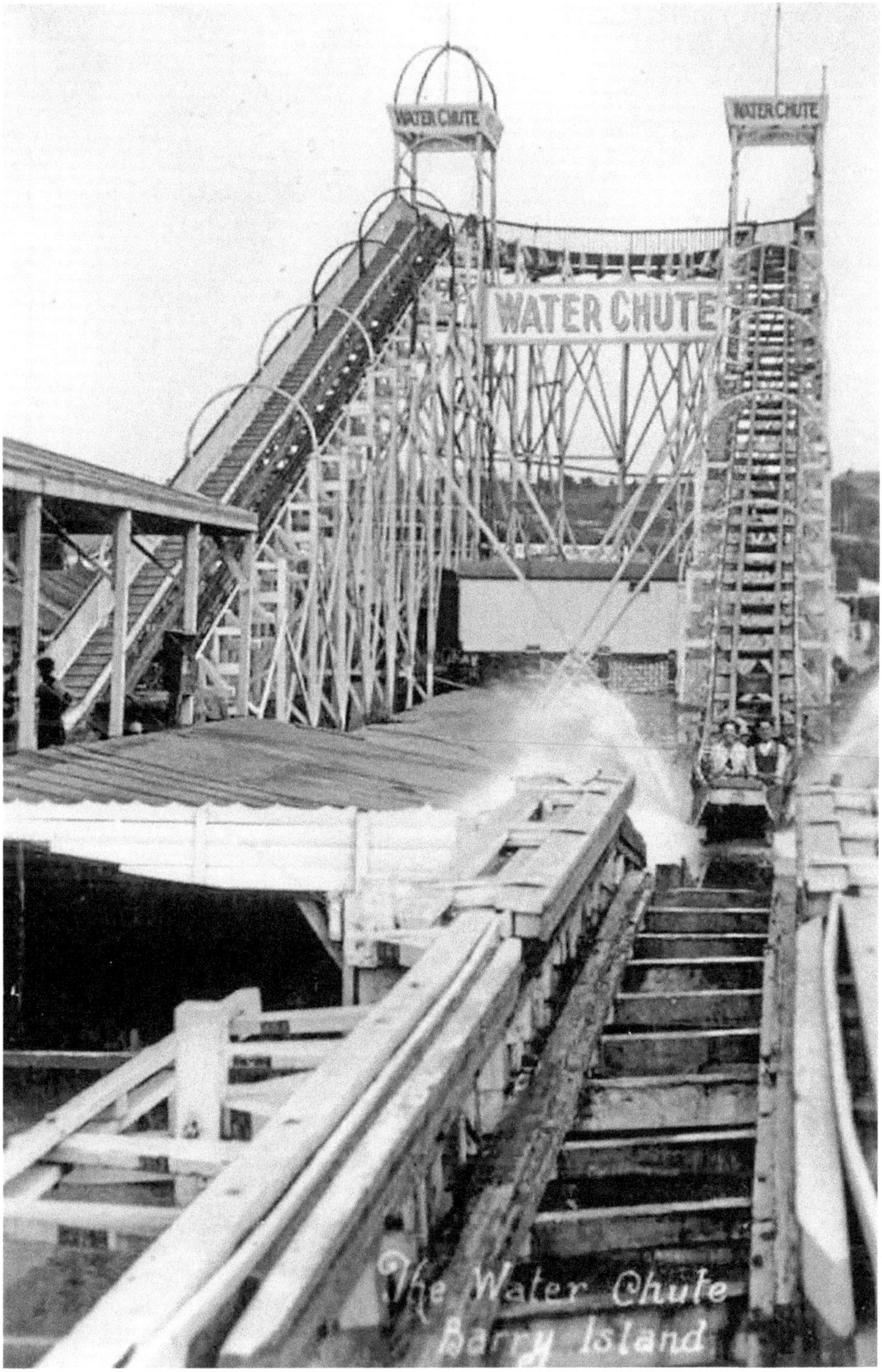

Tourists enjoying an early fairground ride called Water Chute. (Source: Tom Clements.)

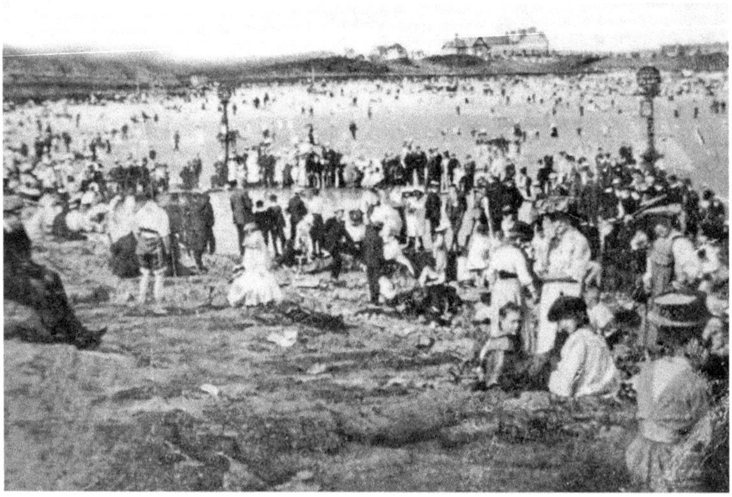

Barry Island as a busy tourist location, early twentieth century. (Source: Tom Clements.)

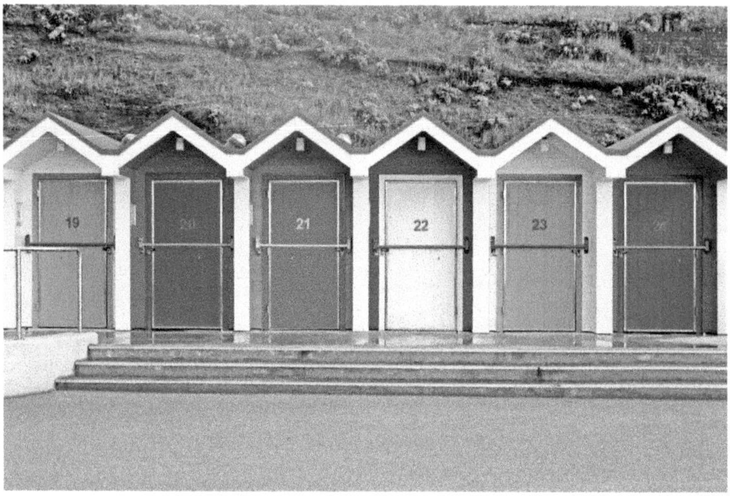

Recent beach huts erected in the eastern shelter and promenade.

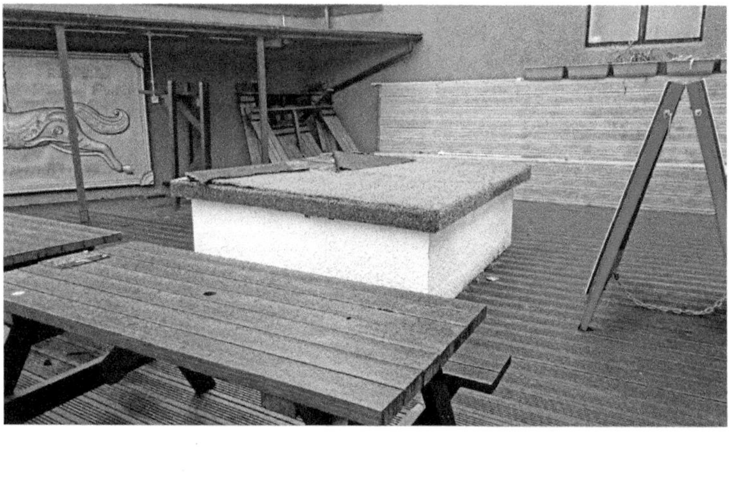

The Roman well as it is today.

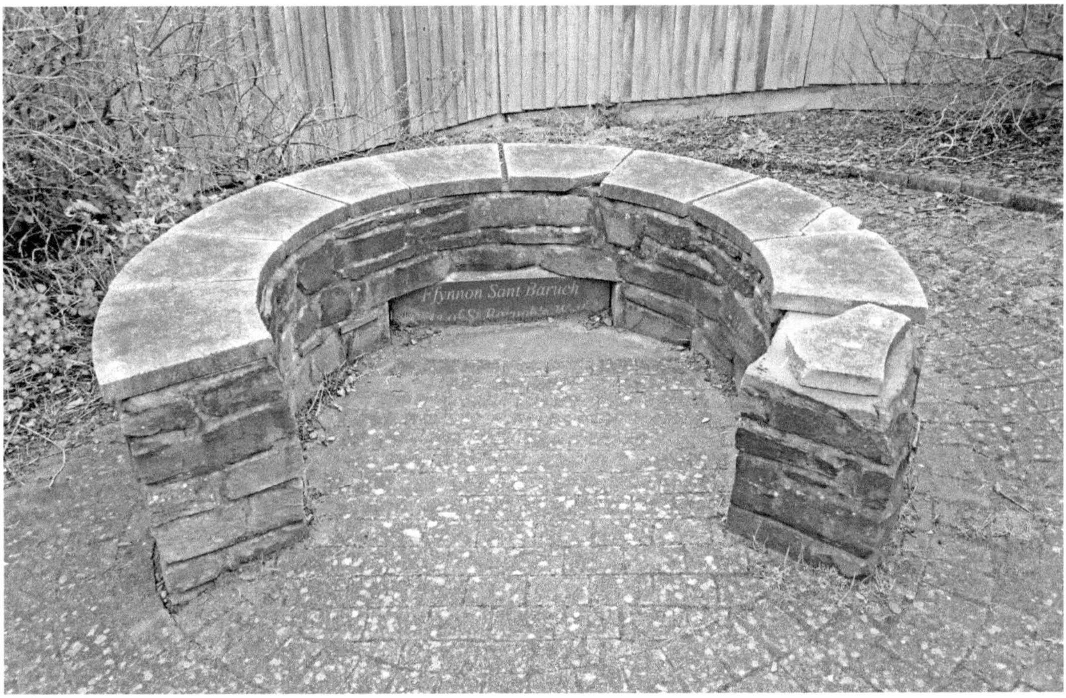

St Barruc's Well as it appears today.

£3-million regeneration scheme subsidised by the Welsh government, which has provided much needed renovation to Barry Island's eastern shelter and promenade – previously neglected for many years and considered an eyesore. In addition, new toilet facilities, a covered amphitheatre, a water-mist feature, landscaped gardens, and a variety of colourful new beach huts have been constructed, greatly enhancing the overall appearance of the eastern promenade – a move that the Welsh government hope will help to stimulate tourism to something approaching Barry Island's zenith during the 1960s.

Both St Barruc's Well and the 'Roman' well have both been capped and now lie in the middle of modern developments. The medieval dwellings thought by Storrie to be the 'Early Abbey' are also gone, as they were destroyed by the development of the fairground. The small seventeenth-century farmhouse with its alleged smugglers' cellars is also gone; it was destroyed with the construction of the Barry Island railway station during the late nineteenth century.

The chapel of St Barruc, however, is still visible and can be visited at any time, as can the remains of two of the barrows on Friars Point. Friars Point House is also still standing, and is now a Grade II-listed building.

Acknowledgements

The authors would like to thank the following people/organisations for permission to use copyright material in this book: thanks to the Cambrian Archaeological Society, the Cardiff Naturalists' Society and British History Online for their kind permissions to reproduce material from their journals and archives. Grateful acknowledgement to Mark Lodwick and the Portable Antiquities Scheme Wales for their permission to reproduce images from their database. Also the Glamorgan Archives for permission to reproduce images from their collection. Photographic contributions are gratefully appreciated from Tom Clements. Every attempt has been made to seek permission for copyright material used in this book. However, if we have inadvertently used copyright material without permission/acknowledgement, we apologise and will make the necessary correction at the first opportunity.

Jonathan and Mark would also like to acknowledge and give thanks to those who have seen fit to help us accomplish writing and researching this book. Thanks to Robert Smith and Colin Lambert for their helpful suggestions and special thanks to Shayne Lewis for his patient editing and time spent proofreading. Also a posthumous acknowledgment to the pioneer archaeologists from the Victorian period who, thanks to their passionate spirit of enquiry, have gleaned and preserved information regarding the majority of Barry Island's archaeological sites and enabled future generations to study and understand them before they were destroyed by modern development.

About the Authors

Jonathan and Mark Lambert are lifelong residents of Barry with a passion for local history and archaeology, both having attended Cardiff University and gaining bachelor degrees in archaeology. Both of the authors have been involved with numerous archaeological projects throughout Glamorgan and beyond and have been writing articles about the Vale of Glamorgan's historical and archaeological heritage for a number of years. Our articles can be viewed online at our Hidden Glamorgan blog (glamorganhistoryandarchaeology .blogspot.co.uk).

Bibliography

Allen, J. R. 'A description of Some Cairns on Barry Island, Glamorganshire', *Archaeologia Cambrensis, Series* IV, No. XIV (1873), pp. 188–91.

Cambrensis. G, *The Itinerary and Description of Wales,* in Rhys E. J. M. (ed.) (New York, 1908).

Fox, A., 'An Account of John Storrie's Excavations on Barry Island in 1894–5'; *Transactions of the Cardiff Naturalists,* 69 (1936), pp. 12–36.

Gerald of Wales, 'Journey Through Wales (1188) and the Description of Wales', Lewis Thorpe (trans. and ed.) in Knight, J. K, Excavations of St Barruc's Chapel Barry Island, *Transactions of the Cardiff Naturalists Society,* 99 (1978), pp. 28–65.

Knight, J., 'Excavations at St Barruc's Chapel, Barry Island, Glamorgan', *Transactions of the Cardiff Naturalists Society,* 99 (1978), pp. 28–65.

Matthews, J. H, 'Custom House Records: Account Books of the Customs Port of Cardiff, 1733–93', *Cardiff Records Volume 2* (Cardiff, 1900), pp. 399–402.

Moore, D., *Barry Centenary Book* (1985).

Morris. R. H, 'Parochialia', *Archaeologia Cambrensis* (1911), pp. 73–4.

'Royal Commission on Ancient and Historical Monuments in Wales', in *An Inventory of the Ancient Monuments in Glamorgan: Volume 1: pre Norman: Part 1: the Stone and Bronze Ages* (Cardiff, 1976).

Storrie, J., *Notes on Excavations made during the Summers of 1894–5, at Barry Island and Ely Race Course, on Lands the Properly of the Right Honourable Lord Windsor* (Cardiff, 1896).

Wade-Evans, '*Vitae Sanctorium Britanniae et Genealogiae*', *Board of Celtic Studies No. 9* (Cardiff, 1946).

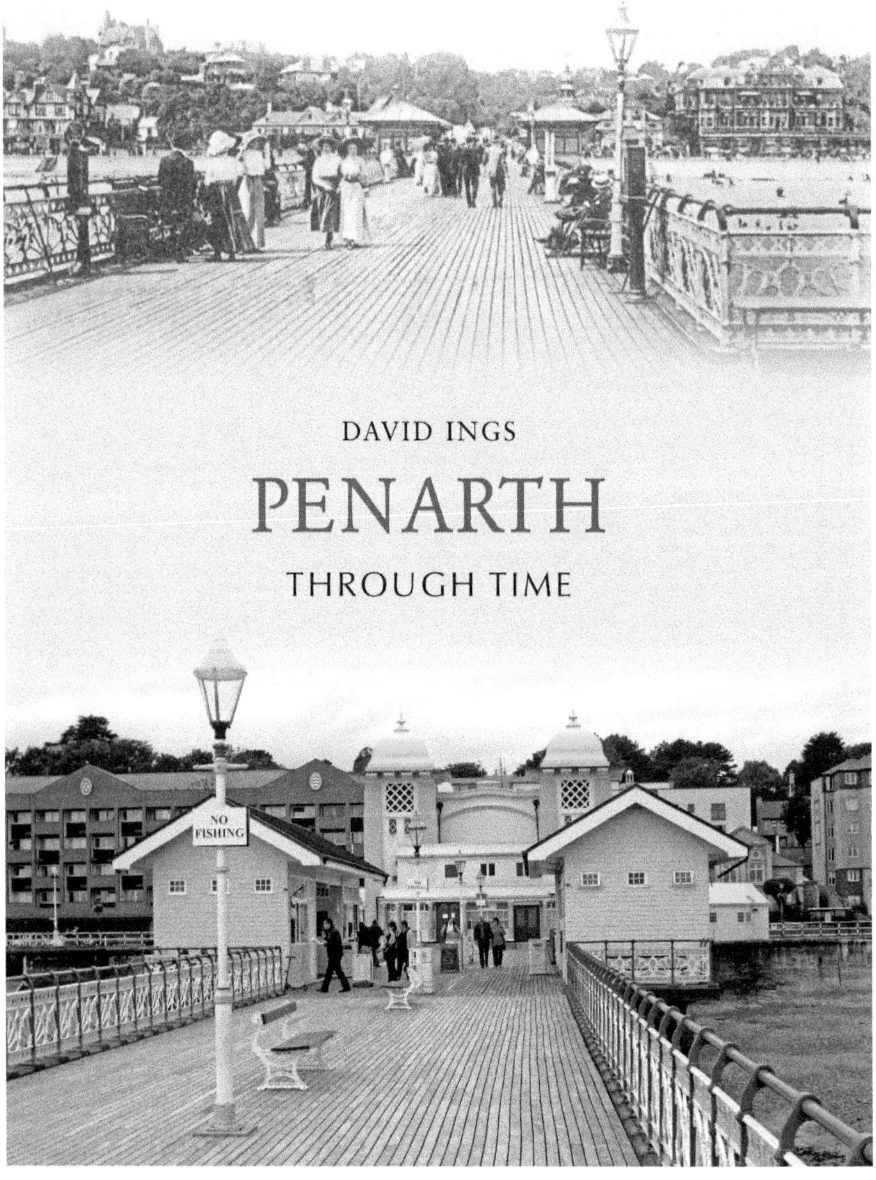
DAVID INGS
PENARTH
THROUGH TIME
NO FISHING

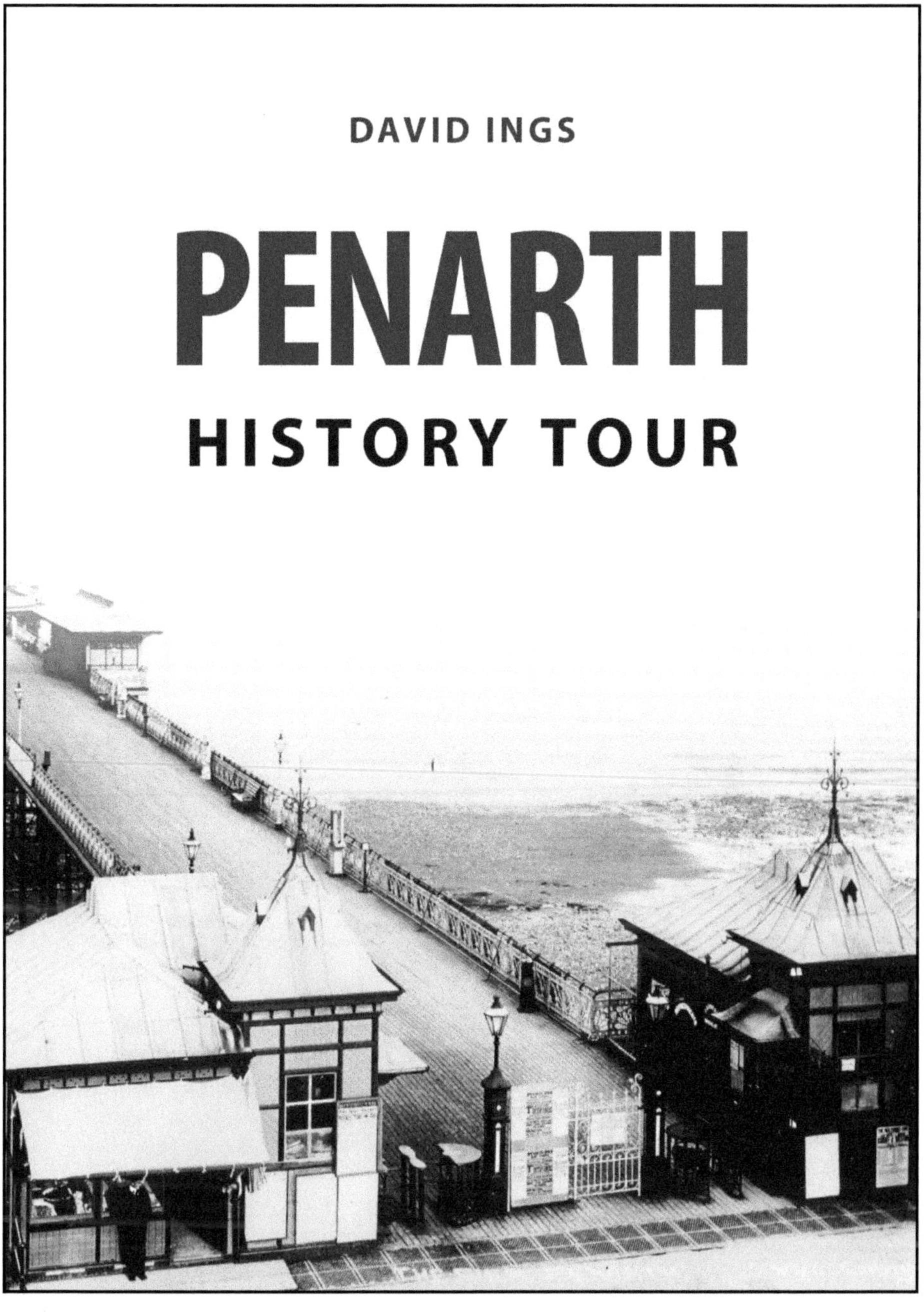
DAVID INGS
PENARTH
HISTORY TOUR